Praise for *Layers*

"As if it weren't enough to be one of the greatest voices on the planet, Sandi is also a great writer who draws you into her struggles and leaves you with God's hope and grace and healing."

—Stephen Arterburn

"Sandi is one of my dearest friends for many reasons. I love her heart, which is rich and full and always thinking of what she could do to bless and encourage someone else. I love her voice, which is like no other. I love her sense of humor, which has rescued me from many a bleak moment. Perhaps more than anything else, I love her vulnerability. Sandi is willing to offer the loaves and fishes of her life and allow Christ to bless them, break them, and feed so many people."

—Sheila Walsh
Author, *Get Off Your Knees and Pray*

"Sandi peels back the layers of her own pain and emotional process to help each of us on our own journey toward health and wholeness. She's real so we can be."

—Mary Graham
President, Women of Faith®

"It blesses me beyond words to see someone who truly is the real deal. Someone who admits that she made poor choices, that she has failed at times, and that loving Jesus does not make you perfect! I know that being transparent may be difficult at first (after all, we have layers placed so perfectly), but the freedom and empowerment that come from being who you truly are—mistakes and all—make the difficult seem easier. Our layers, whether brought on by us or given to us, don't have to be more than they are. I always say that my poor choices are neither to be worn like a scarlet letter nor to be held high like a medal of honor. They are just choices, given to the Lord for Him to use for His glory! Thank you, Sandi, for giving Him all the glory and for allowing the world to see how beautiful a woman can be without all the layers of life holding her down!"

—Tracy Elliott
Mrs. Texas 2006 and Author, *Unbroken*

"Sandi's book is a brilliant as well as tender account of the layers of protection she's used for years to keep her core pain from being seen by anyone, including herself. I so respect her determination to peel back those layers and get acquainted with the beautiful little blonde Sandi just waiting to be discovered. You will love this highly personal journey Sandi invites us to take with her. You will also love knowing there's hope for all of us multilayered persons."

—Marilyn Meberg
Women of Faith® Speaker and
Author, *Love Me, Never Leave Me*

"Sandi Patty's meteoric rise as a popular vocalist was fueled by soaring tunes declaring the glory of God. The astonishing range and sheer power of her voice took our breath away. But as the circumstances of her personal life began to change, her musical signature did as well. Her repertoire deepened with a catalog of thoughtful lyrics that speak of God's grace—a grace made all the more extraordinary by the realization that He knows *everything* about us. In *Layers*, Sandi tells the story of peeling back the layers of her own heart and soul, a painful peeling at times, but a peeling without which grace cannot be fully understood or received. *Layers* challenges all of us to be honest, knowing that the truth always heals . . . even when it's hard to bear."

—Jim Lyon
Pastor, Madison Park Church of God

Layers

Uncovering and Celebrating
God's Original Idea of You

Sandi Patty

Thomas Nelson

Since 1798

NASHVILLE DALLAS MEXICO CITY RIO DE JANEIRO BEIJING

Published in Nashville, Tennessee, by Thomas Nelson. Thomas Nelson is a registered trademark of Thomas Nelson, Inc.

Thomas Nelson, Inc., titles may be purchased in bulk for educational, business, fund-raising, or sales promotional use. For information, please e-mail SpecialMarkets@ThomasNelson.com.

Library of Congress Cataloging-in-Publication Data

Patty, Sandi, 1956–
    Layers : uncovering and celebrating God's original idea of you / Sandi Patty.
      p. cm.
    Includes bibliographical references.
    ISBN 978-0-7852-2829-5 (hardcover)
    1. Christian women—Religious life. 2. Self-actualization
(Psychology)—Religious aspects—Christianity. 3. Patty, Sandi, 1956–
I. Title.
BV4527.P3865 2008
248.8'43—dc22

2008005159

Printed in the United States of America

08 09 10 11 12 QW 9 8 7 6 5 4 3

To my husband and best friend,

Don,

who has layered me

with the love of Christ.

LAYERS

Buried deep beneath this skin lies a child full of hope.
Let her out, let her soar.
Why do you cover her with your shame, why do you layer
  her with your guilt?
Tell her she's been set free, tell her she's okay,
Tell her she doesn't have to be ashamed and hide behind
  the armor of false protection and guilt.
She trusts in the lie that says she will never be safe
And that she will never know freedom and love and peace,
But you can tell her, you can give her wings,
You can help her speak.
She shies as she listens—she can't believe it's true
No more hiding, no more layers of the lies that cage her in
She's a beauty, she's a princess,
She's a woman-child with much to say.
Just knowing, she stands taller, she stands prouder,
She stands sure.
All she needed was permission to lose the cravings of her shame.
It was she who held on tight and not the chains that bound.
I can see her in the distance, running, arms open wide,
Longing to be known, longing to be loved, longing to belong,
Craving union with her soul, craving fullness of contentment,
And I hold her in my heart, and I welcome my old friend.

It is this that leaves her full
Coming home to all of me, more of me, less of me,
And the layers of protection begin to melt away on sight,
No longer needed as a buffer,
She walks naked into the light, exposing all of her to His
    mercy and His love
Not holding back, she dances into my arms of love.

—SANDI PATTY, 2006

CONTENTS

ACKNOWLEDGMENTS

I must first and foremost thank my heavenly Father for patiently peeling and healing the layers of my life.

I am so very grateful to my family for practicing grace with me every day.

I love my Women of Faith family, and I thank you from the bottom of my soul for giving my heart—scars and all—a home.

Thank you, Sue Ann Jones, for listening, hearing, and helping me tell my story.

And thank you to Thomas Nelson, especially to Debbie Wickwire, for literally crossing every T and dotting every I.

So What Do You Need?

> *Pure grace and nothing but grace be with*
> *all who love our Master, Jesus Christ.*
>
> —EPHESIANS 6:24 MSG

Our son Sam, then eleven, started playing football last year. One fall Saturday he hopped in the car beside Don, and off they went to the first practice. I dropped by the sports field a little while later, eager to see my sports-loving boy discover a new venue for showing off his athletic talent.

It took me a while to pick him out of the crowd of kids lining up head-to-head then charging at each other at full speed. From a distance they all looked alike because they were all wearing top-heavy helmets and enormous shoulder pads. Eventually, though, one of the helmets turned my way, and a few minutes later Sam came trotting over to me.

"Sam, is that *you?*" I said, my eyes wide in mock amazement.

"Mom, it feels like my head's gonna fall off," he muttered. "I can barely move! I feel like a giant hot dog stuffed in a too-small bun."

I laughed and patted him on the head—or, rather, the helmet. "I know it feels awkward, sugar, but you've gotta wear it. It protects you and keeps you from getting hurt."

"I know, I know," Sam groaned. "That's what the coaches say. They say we have to practice with this stuff on so we're used to wearing it when we have a real game." He turned and lumbered back onto the field. Halfway there he turned and looked like he might be blowing me a kiss—but the face guard got in the way.

That conversation occurred several months ago, and let me just tell you that since that first practice, our Sam has become quite a dynamo out there on the gridiron. When it's his turn to run out on the field, he pulls on that helmet and tears off toward the action like a gladiator eager to face the lions.

Sam needs that protective equipment when he's playing football. As his mother, I'm glad to see his precious head encased in the helmet and his growing shoulders protected by pads when he's on the field and his opponents seem determined to run him down and flatten him. I like it that he's wearing extra layers when he's "doing battle." In fact, if I had my way, he'd probably be wearing a double helmet and triple total-body pads!

But when he comes home, I want my *real* Sam back—the handsome, slim, tenderhearted guy, now a sixth-grader, who snuggles up to me on the couch, wiggles under my arm for a back rub while I'm working in the kitchen, and smiles when I playfully rub his curly hair.

Sam has learned that out on the football field, he needs thick, hard layers of protection to keep from getting hurt. But he has also learned that when he's home, in the heart of his family, the best cuddling, greatest affection, and most rewarding experiences of feeling loved come when he peels off the layers and becomes real again, like he was before he started playing football.

Hmmm. I stand looking at the sweaty pads and discarded helmet Sam dropped beside his workout clothes in the laundry room and can't help but wish I could shed my own protective layers and become real again as easily as Sam does.

LAYERS? WHAT LAYERS?

When we're kids, layers may be protective sports gear or some kind of uniform or playtime costume that we can easily cast aside when we step out of our extracurricular roles and come home to our real lives, like Sam did with his football equipment. As children at home with our families, we can be ourselves, knowing we'll be loved and protected by our parents and siblings, no matter what. We don't have to pretend to be something we're not. We don't have to wear protective padding or costumes. We can just be ourselves.

At least, that's the way it's supposed to be. That's the way most of us start out. But inevitably, something happens that changes our blissfully vulnerable and honest existence. Something hurts us—something we may not even remember fully as adults yet can't quite forget—and gradually we build up layers of protection to keep us from getting hurt again.

The hurt may be caused by something small, like an obnoxious schoolmate loudly scoffing at the holes in our shoes or our poor grade on the math test. Or it can be something big, such as abandonment, physical injury, or sexual abuse. Whatever hurts us can cause us to pull on layers that we hope, consciously or subconsciously, will protect us or keep the hurt from happening again. These layers may be visible in our physical bodies (like layers of fat or fingernails bitten to the quick). Or they may exist as outward behaviors (like layers of compulsiveness or unprovoked anger) that push others away from us. Or the layers may exist invisibly in our innermost thoughts (when we tell ourselves we're unfit, unworthy, or unlovable), "protecting" us from others that we assume feel the same way about us.

> *But inevitably, something happens that changes our blissfully vulnerable and honest existence. Something hurts us.*

Your story may be very different from mine, and your layers may be protecting you from other kinds of situations or scenarios or secrets you've hidden even from yourself. Maybe you're carrying layers of fear, hiding the false belief that you're not good enough, smart enough, slim enough, or interesting enough. Whatever layers are weighing you down, my prayer is that God will deal with you the same way He's dealing with me. Tenderly, graciously, lovingly, He's helping me peel those layers away to find and celebrate the original me He created. That's the journey I'm inviting you to share with me as we move from page to page of this book . . . and from season to season of our lives.

In the beginning, when layers are new, we may be able to lay them aside and still be our authentic, genuine selves when we're with those closest to us, the ones we still trust. Maybe we pull on our layers only when we're around certain people or in specific situations. But whenever we allow the protective layers to remain in place, they grow ever more strongly attached to us. Pretty soon they feel so familiar we may forget what caused us to create them in the first place. We start thinking they're real. We start believing what we see in the mirror or hear ourselves saying aloud to others or silently to ourselves. Eventually the layers become barricades, preventing us from feeling loved as we want and need.

Meanwhile, there sits the God of the universe, who created us to be His beloved children, longing to pull us into His loving embrace, rub us on the head, pat us on the back, and tell us how wonderful we are . . . while we stand there, helmeted by stubbornness, padded by shame, armored by failure, and hardened by guilt, wanting with everything in our being to shed the layers and fall blissfully and unburdened into His everlasting arms.

But try as we might, we can't do it. We can't loosen the layers and step free of the protective barricade we've built around ourselves.

At least we can't do it alone.

THE DIFFERENT SOUNDS OF THE SAME DOORS, SLAMMING

Fifteen years ago, I found myself encumbered by so many layers of what I've come to think of as "false-Sandiness" that I no longer knew who the real Sandi was. The public knew my façade as a smiling wife, a devoted mother of four kids, and a successful Christian recording artist. But beneath those layers—some visible, some not—I was miserable. Separated from my husband and in love with another man, Don, I took a headlong plunge off the pedestal of Christian celebrity and eventually ended up at the front door of a mental health facility. I needed help, and I needed it *badly*.

I had expected the facility to be a rather exclusive spa, a posh country-club kind of place with thick terry-cloth robes and bedtime mints on the pillows. It was, instead, a rather bleak-looking hospital, where I had a two-week-long appointment in the psych ward.

I didn't like what I saw, and I didn't want to be there. I stood at that front door a moment, deciding what to do. On that side of the door, I had a choice. But I wasn't sure I would still have a choice once I got inside.

After a while, I clinched my jaw, hardened my resolve, and walked through the door. I jumped as it slammed shut behind me. I walked through another door, and it, too, slammed behind me. I got in the elevator, and the doors closed. *They're probably locked so I can't go back down,* I mused to myself sarcastically. The elevator took me to the floor where my appointment was scheduled. The elevator opened, and there stood my therapist, smiling warmly. I fell into her arms like a child running to Mom with a scraped knee. We turned toward the psych department, and as we approached, I read the signs warning that the doors were to remain locked at all times.

I felt my blood pressure rising.

We pushed through the doors and they whooshed shut behind us. I flinched as I heard them locking. She led me into another area, and as we passed through those doors, they locked behind us too.

Finally we arrived in her office. By then I was agitated and wiping away tears. I felt as though I'd arrived in a prison. "Are you okay?" the therapist asked me, dropping her head to look into my downcast eyes.

"No," I answered, probably too harshly. "I'm *not* okay."

Then she asked me something that's now become a part of my everyday vernacular: "So, what do you need?"

Her question let me know she was sensitive to my feelings, but at the same time she was putting responsibility on *me* to find the words to express what I was feeling.

"I need to get out of here," I said bluntly.

"Okay," she said, nodding sympathetically.

"But I can't. The doors are all locked."

"They can be unlocked."

Incredibly, I argued with her. "No, they can't. It's a rule. They can't be unlocked."

She walked around her desk, stuck her head through the office doorway, and asked someone at the nurses' station to unlock the doors.

I said, "You're telling me I can just walk out of here?"

"Yes," she answered. "That's what I'm telling you."

So I left. I steamed out of her office, walked through all the suddenly unlocked doors, tapped my foot as I waited for the elevator and, a few minutes later, stepped outside into the cold air and the snow that was just beginning to fall. I was surprised to see that the therapist had followed me. We stood there on the hospital's front lawn, silently facing each other. I was out of breath and crying, worked up both by my hurried exit and by the tornado of emotions tearing through my mind.

"So, what do you need now?" she asked calmly.

I glared at her a moment, angrily wiping away tears. "I need to go back inside and get to work," I said.

She smiled and nodded. "Okay then. Let's go."

We walked together back into the hospital, back through all the doors that once again locked behind us as we stepped through. Amazingly, those same doors sounded completely different that third time through. What had felt and sounded at first like a prison now felt as welcoming as a refuge. What at first sounded like a trap now had the ring of tenderness as

I heard those doors close in safety. And I had to ask myself . . . what changed? The doors and locks certainly hadn't changed. The hospital was still a hospital. My therapist was still my therapist.

What had changed was me. Now I understood that I had a choice—and I was choosing to view my world at that moment through different lenses. The place that at first had felt like a prison had, in an instant, become my protection. I chose to stay, knowing it was a place where I could safely begin to heal.

> *What at first sounded like a trap now had the ring of tenderness as I heard those doors close in safety.*

It may sound strange—after all, I had chosen to go to the facility for treatment in the first place—but knowing I could still choose to stay or go once I got there had made the difference.

THE IRONIC CONTRADICTION

Like the doors of that hospital, emotional layers can have contradictory sounds or functions. Let's face it. We all have layers that we hide behind at one time or another. They may feel imprisoning—or protective. They may start out as something good and turn into something bad. Or we may decide they're something that's always bad—and then find out they're sometimes necessary for emotional or even physical survival.

The thing about layers is we need to recognize them for what they are and learn that we can *choose* how we deal with them. Some of them need to be done away with entirely. Others are needed to protect us when we're genuinely threatened by physical, emotional, or spiritual harm. (After all, Ephesians 6:11 tells us to "put on the full armor of God so that you can take your stand against the devil's schemes.")

The important thing is, though, that *nothing* should stand between us and the God who created us. To enjoy His richest blessings for our lives, we must come to Him constantly as our real, authentic selves, even when it's not what *we* consider pretty or together.

The thing about layers is we need to recognize them for what they are and learn that we can choose how we deal with them.

It's certainly nothing to brag about, but I know all about layers from personal experience. In this book I'll share with you how God has penetrated the destructive layers I've created through my many failures over the years. I hope my story will encourage you to recognize your own protective and imprisoning layers and then to ask for God's help in unwrapping the wonderful, *real* person He created you to be.

Once you discover that wonderful creation, I think you'll also realize, as I have, that the layer all of us need most is the wonderful gift of His grace. That grace means He wraps our vulnerable, failure-prone selves in His eternal love and promises to forgive us, no matter what layers of sin and mistakes we try to cling to. And in that soothing, sustaining layer of grace, we find perpetual refuge.

Maybe we share some of the same layers. Maybe you've struggled with your weight for a thousand years, as I have. Maybe you've built up a layer of defensiveness in response to harsh criticism following devastating failures. Maybe, like me, you're the victim of some kind of abuse (in my case, sexual abuse by a female babysitter), and you've unknowingly developed layers of behaviors in response to that situation.

Or perhaps you struggle with other kinds of layers: alcohol or drug addiction, pointless busyness, poor choices in relationships, illicit sex, uncontrollable gambling, compulsive shopping, explosive anger, or unrealistic perfectionism. We layer ourselves with all sorts of things, whatever we can find that will ease the pain, embarrassment, excesses, guilt, and failures we've somehow accumulated in response to hurtful situations in our lives.

RECOGNIZING OUR LAYERS
AND COPING WITH THEIR EFFECTS

We first need to recognize our layers. Then we can gather information and gain understanding about how those layers affect us—and how we can, with God's help (and perhaps professional help too) cope with them, either by removing them entirely or learning how to use them appropriately. Finally, we'll celebrate what we've accomplished and then move on to the next layer—because inevitably, there *will* be another one. But the more we get reacquainted with the original person God created us to be, the easier it gets to see through what's happening and shed those layers that prevent us from living the abundantly rewarding life He wants us to have. He told us that in Matthew 6:33: "Seek first the kingdom of God and His righteousness, and all these things shall be added to you" (NKJV).

But the more we get reacquainted with the original person God created us to be, the easier it gets to . . . shed those layers that prevent us from living the abundantly rewarding life He wants us to have.

That is where I realize I must begin—to seek Him first and foremost. Then the other things will fall into place. I desire to know Christ. I *want* to know Christ.

I want to know Him the way the apostle Paul did when he wrote to the Philippians, "I gave up all that inferior stuff so I could know Christ personally, experience his resurrection power, be a partner in his suffering, and go all the way with him to death itself" (3:10 MSG).

If I begin there, partnering with Jesus, knowing Him personally and constantly keeping my eye on that goal, then everything else makes more sense. It is the cornerstone of who I am; it is the very foundation upon which everything else lays. If I *don't* begin there, with Christ, the rest of my world makes no sense.

It is a daily, sometimes hourly, decision, desire, and choice to say, "I seek You *first* today, Lord." It is a version of what Jesus Himself prayed: "This is the real and eternal life: That they know you, the one and only true God, and Jesus Christ, whom you sent" (John 17:3 MSG).

I've left a lot of layers behind since that day at the hospital so long ago. (Oh, don't worry, there are still plenty more to work through.) And believe me; some of those experiences haven't been pretty. But neither were the hurts that painted those layers onto my psyche. I'm sharing my story here, hoping it will encourage you to look at your own life and ask God's help in penetrating through anything that's keeping you from knowing yourself as He knows you: as a wonderfully amazing being surrounded by love and grace.

Recognizing my own layers meant revisiting an episode of abuse that occurred when I was six years old. I'll tell you about the incident now, to get the ugly event out of the way. Then I'll share with you, here and in later chapters, some of the layers I learned to recognize as a result of the emotional hurt I suffered.

I'd love to also write a chapter saying, "I got rid of my destructive layers, and so can you." But that verb tense would be wrong. Instead, this book, like my life, will share what is—and what will always be—a work in progress.

The truth is, I'm still getting rid of my destructive layers. It is a lifelong process. Come along, and we'll work at this challenge together.

Many of my layers began with the childhood abuse. In therapy, it became obvious that was the place to start. My godly parents reared my two brothers and me with all the love in the world. My father is a retired minister, my mother a talented pianist, and together they have devoted their lives to the gospel—and to their family. We kids were affirmed and nurtured every day of our lives, and when we got older we spent our summers happily traveling the country presenting gospel music programs as a family. I don't mean to say we were the perfect family. In every family there are always issues to be worked through, and later I'll share how I identified, during my unlayering, how one attitude issue accidentally occurred and followed me into adulthood. But I can say that, looking back over my life, I am grateful for all of the love and support my parents have given me. It remains a foundation for my life.

When we were little, however, Mom and Dad's musical ministry meant they occasionally had to leave us kids behind while they spent a week (never more) on the road, touring with a quartet that my dad was part of. My mother was the pianist, and family friend and gifted musician Doug Oldham was one of the other members of the quartet. They had formed this quartet while they were in college and stayed together for several years afterward.

When I was six, they had to be away from home several

days on a concert tour. They left my brothers with some close neighborhood friends, and they left me with a trusted friend from church. I remember how sweetly the woman spoke to my parents and me as we arrived at her house that day. But as soon as Mom and Dad had said good-bye and disappeared down the street, she became a completely different person, frighteningly cold and bitter.

During that long, terrifying week, the woman tended to my needs but never showed me any real warmth or kindness. The highlight of each day came at bedtime, when she gave me milk and cookies. Then came the darkness.

Therapists confirm that what happened to me was sexual abuse even though I wasn't raped or physically hurt. I was repeatedly touched in inappropriate ways—and, in the process, traumatized. The nightly incidents of abuse were so confusing and frightening to my young, innocent mind that I could not speak or cry out to try and stop them. I didn't understand why it was happening, but like most victims of abuse, I assumed I must have done something really bad to deserve such treatment. That's why abuse victims often don't tell anyone about the abuse. That's why I didn't tell my parents when they picked me up at the end of the week. I was overjoyed to see them but didn't say anything about what the woman had done to me.

In my childish mind (and I've learned this is a common, unconscious way abused children think), I reasoned that adults don't do bad things to children, so I surely had done something terribly wrong to have caused the babysitter to treat me in such a harsh and humiliating way. I didn't know what I'd done to deserve such treatment, but whatever it was, I certainly didn't want my parents to find out. I might get into even bigger trouble.

Years later, my talented, caring Christian therapists helped me sort out the twisted childhood reasoning that had caused me to blame myself for the abuse. They helped me understand that choice becomes very critical for many abuse victims because choice was taken away by the abuser. The victim has no choice; he or she is helpless at the hands of the abuser.

GETTING UNSTUCK

I've learned that choice can be an especially big deal to those who were abused at an early age. We may feel panicky if we think we have no choice, as I did when I heard the hospital doors locking behind me. Or, ironically, we may panic if we *do* have a choice; we get stuck, unable to choose because not knowing which choice is right triggers that memory of our mistaken childhood feelings when we didn't know what we'd done wrong to prompt the abuse. So we subconsciously think maybe it's better just not to choose at all—which leaves us feeling stuck and helpless, which, ironically, is the same way we may feel when we *don't* have a choice. In my case, I have some kind of confusing fear that I have to know *everything* about something before I can make a choice. And, of course, no one can know *everything* about *anything*.

I clearly remember when John (my former husband) and I were first divorced, and we were getting used to shuffling the kids back and forth from one house to another. I was used to being with my kids 24/7, and it was very difficult for me to adjust to their leaving and going to their dad's house for a few days.

On one weekend in particular my current situation collided with my childhood fears. My kids had gone to their dad's, and I was alone in my house. Suddenly, seemingly out of the blue, I was gripped with panic and fear. I began to ask these questions in my mind: *What if my kids need me and they can't call me? What if something terrible is happening and they can't get to me? What if I can't get to them if I need them? What if they didn't have a choice? What if I didn't have a choice?*

Thank God for my girlfriends, whom I immediately called. As I began to talk to my Ya-Yas, they

> My girlfriends knew that asking questions was the place to begin.

were insightful enough to see what was happening. They began to ask me, "What are you feeling right now? Do you remember feeling like this before?"

My girlfriends knew that asking questions was the place to begin. And as the conversation began to unfold, I realized that while the adult Sandi was missing her kids, the child Sandi was panicked because she couldn't get to her parents—and the child Sandi *did* have bad things happen to her.

Once I realized that these intense, overwhelming feelings were coming from my childhood, I was able to put my current sadness in perspective. Very often something in the present will trigger a past layer covered deep from the past. As we begin to uncover those layers, we can begin to bring healing to those old wounds.

See why we may need help in recognizing and coping with these layers we wrap ourselves in? It's not a snap-your-fingers kind of deal. It takes some work, some prayer—and God. The choice thing is just one of the layers I'm dealing with. Because ultimately I have to choose to believe (and accept) that God loves me . . . just as I am . . . right now. Oh yeah, this choice thing is a big one. In the chapters to come, I'll share some others.

I've identified them—and I'm still on the lookout for them—thanks to the help of those Christian mental health professionals at the New Life Center fifteen years ago and others since then. At the hospital, they encouraged and helped me—for the first time—to describe the abuse to my parents, who were understandably horrified and heartbroken by what had happened to me. Then those same therapists helped me identify the protective—and imprisoning— layers I'd wrapped around myself in response to the abuse and to other hurts I've endured. With their help—and the help of my family, my church, and my friends—I'm now laying claim to God's grace that makes all those destructive layers totally unnecessary.

It makes *your* destructive layers unnecessary too. That's what this book is all about.

So what do I need now?

I need to choose to lose the layers and wrap myself in God's grace. "For it is by grace you have been saved, through faith—and this not from yourselves, it is the gift of God" (Ephesians 2:8).

So what do you need now?

I need _____

_____

_____

_____

_____

2

Outsmarting the Mirror

Your beauty should not come from outward adornment . . .
Instead, it should be that of your inner self.

—1 PETER 3:3—4

I've been on every diet and weight-loss plan ever invented. That's why I tell audiences that in my closet I have sizes 14, 16, 18, and none-of-your-business. I hate being heavy, and I've tried dozens of ways to take off pounds. The problem is that food is so comforting to me. In fact, when I started stressing out about making myself sit down to write this book as the deadline loomed, I ended up in the kitchen making chocolate chip cookies! Somehow the stress eased a bit as I tasted that wonderful blend of brown sugar, shortening, flour, and chocolate moving around my mouth.

A poor self-image is one of the layers that landed in my life after the childhood abuse, and I've struggled with it for decades. I know now that at age six I had the looks that triggered those dark and evil urges in my abuser. I was cute—blonde-haired, blue-eyed, active, and happy. After the traumatizing incidents, I entered a lifetime of inner conflict about my appearance. I wanted to always look my best; I wanted to be pretty, as all girls do. But subconsciously I layered myself with fears that looking pretty might cause the abuse to happen again.

Also tied to this layering was the fact that during the week of nightly abuse at the babysitter's hands, the only good thing that happened was the cookies and milk she fed me at bedtime. That familiar food comforted me during a toxic and stressful situation, just as it still does today.

So I eat. And I gain. Then I try to eat less and lose. But it's oh, so hard. When I called my friend Carolyn for encouragement during my current dieting attempt, she said, "Of course it's hard, Sandi. You're losing your best friend. Food has always been there for you to comfort you and reassure you. When you feel anxious or stressed, it makes you feel better."

A poor self-image is one of the layers that landed in my life after the childhood abuse, and I've struggled with it for decades.

Someone else likened dieting to going through a divorce, and I think it's a fitting analogy. Those of us who have been through a divorce and who have children know that even though you're ending something that has been an everyday, vital part of your life, you can't cut yourself off from your former spouse completely. You have to deal with that other person again and again as you share custody, arrange visitations, and rear your children. When you go on a diet, you're ending the previous long-term relationship you've had with food, but you can't cut it out of your life completely. You can't sign some papers, move to another state, and never see food again. We've got to have it. It's meant to sustain life. We love it—and we hate it too. What we have to do is redefine our relationship, acknowledging that there may be some grieving involved as well as a sense of loss.

FINDING A WORKABLE SOLUTION

Earlier I mentioned how the issue of choice is a difficult one for me, as it is with many abuse victims, and how easy it is to get stuck in the muck of indecision. Recently that indecisive emotional layer blended with my poor-self-image layer to create a doubly difficult situation. But when I took a step back and recognized what was happening, I managed to work through those layers to find a workable solution.

As a step toward improving my health (and, I hope, losing weight), I signed up with a personal trainer last year. I didn't have any dreams of becoming Miss America. In fact, my goal had nothing at all to do with physical improvements. My goal was simply to finish all twelve sessions I'd contracted for, without quitting!

Things started off fine. I enjoyed the workouts and didn't cancel or even reschedule a single session. At about the same time, I'd started on the Zone Diet, based on the best-selling 1995 book by Dr. Barry Sears. I'd lost weight on the Zone before, and I felt good about trying it again.

Then at one of the workout sessions, my trainer handed me a piece of paper and said it was an "eating" program he wanted me to try. Well, there was the choice. I could have said to him, "You know, your plan is probably good, but I'm really comfortable with the Zone, so I'm going to stick with that."

Wouldn't that have been easy? No big deal for most people, right?

Maybe for *most* people but not for me.

It came down to the fact that I needed to make a choice, and I didn't trust myself to choose the right thing. Maybe I was remembering the times in my life when I had made a choice and had gotten into trouble. I know it sounds ridiculous (and just writing these words makes the whole thing appear downright stupid), but I got stuck there in that muck of choosing the Zone or the trainer's eating plan.

I was stuck, and I didn't know what to do. And when I'm stuck I fall backward into my old destructive ways. I started grabbing any food that was handy. As Dr. Henry Cloud says, when we deviate from our plan, we revert to our old patterns. My old patterns of eating brought me back to those old, familiar feelings of being disappointed in myself, degrading myself (*You idiot! Why are you eating that?*), and starting the food-is-comfort cycle all over again.

Fortunately, I still had enough sense to pray the two-word prayer that's become a total-life mantra for me: "God, help!"

Okay, so it's not the most eloquent prayer. But it's one I

pray daily, sometimes hourly, and it brings the wisdom of
the Creator of the universe into my little dilemma, whatever
it is.

Well, no sooner had I prayed that prayer when the doorbell rang. (I must admit, God doesn't always answer this
quickly, but that day He apparently had an opening in His
schedule.) It was the UPS guy, and he was delivering a huge box . . .
of food!

A month earlier, one of the kids had asked me to order some
NutriSystem products, hoping to do a quick little slim-down before
the current college session started.
I thought I had just ordered four
weeks' worth of food, but apparently I had clicked on the
auto-delivery button, and now there stood the UPS guy, waiting for my signature—while the NutriSystem kid had already
left for college.

> *No sooner had
> I prayed that
> prayer than the
> doorbell rang.*

Just what I needed: another choice.

Frankly, my first choice was to be ticked off at someone: either my child (who hadn't done the ordering, I had)
or NutriSystem (who had, no doubt, simply done what I'd
inadvertently requested). Both of *those* choices made about
as much sense as being stuck over which diet to choose, so
I was able to move on to the bigger issue: what to do with
that big box of stuff.

I stood there in the entryway, looking at it. Then I realized

I'd carried my cordless phone with me when I answered the door. I called Carolyn and told her the whole stupid story. (Carolyn is not only my friend, she's my awesome life coach, and she totally "gets it." She's a wonderful help and encourager to me—and many others. You'll find the Web address for her practice in the resources section at the back of this book.)

"Sandi, did you say you had just asked God for help, and then the doorbell rang?" Carolyn said to me that morning.

"Yeah, that's what happened," I answered.

There was a pause. "Well . . . let me tell you something I did that I haven't mentioned to you," she said. "Please don't think I'm making this up because I'm not. But I know your struggle in this area."

I couldn't imagine what she was going to say. "Two weeks ago I did some investigating online, and I was thinking of all your traveling, how you spend so much time away from home, and I felt at the time that NutriSystem might be a good idea for you. But I didn't tell you because I know how you also struggle with choices, and I didn't want to suggest it to you until I'd checked into it. So I ordered it myself for a couple of weeks to try it out, just to see if I thought it would work for you," she said.

"Carolyn, come on. You're a size 4!" I interrupted.

"Well, I just wanted to try it out and see if it might be something I would suggest to you, and you know, I think it might be good for you. Everything is right there, and you can throw it in your suitcase and take it with you."

What an amazing "God moment" that was for me.

Carolyn continued, "But I'm wondering . . . how do you feel about NutriSystem telling you what to eat? Because I know how that would mean you lose the choice thing."

"I'm really okay with that," I answered, "because I'm *choosing* NutriSystem from these three different dieting options. I'm gonna give it a try."

Two months into the program, I still was not quite ready to borrow any of Carolyn's size 4 clothes (and probably never will be!), but I'm happy with the plan, and I'm pretty much sticking to it.

If you're someone who also has a hard time making decisions, take a moment to consider where that layer of chronic indecision may be coming from. Ask God for help in discerning the right way to go, then wait for a light-bulb to go on in your mind (or listen for your doorbell to ring!).

> *Ask God for help in discerning the right way to go, then . . . listen for your doorbell to ring!*

One single mom said she fretted terribly over decisions, especially those affecting her children's lives. She trained herself to use a three-step process that helped her get unstuck when she felt trapped by indecision. First, she sets a specific time limit for gathering information about the topic (anything from a few minutes to a week). Next, she sets aside another block of time, a few minutes or a couple of hours, to spend alone with God, reading His

Word, praying and opening her heart and mind to His guidance. "Then," she said, "I *decide*, knowing I've done my homework and asked God to help me. And once I've made that decision, I don't worry about it any longer but move forward with confidence, knowing God's going to help me again to make it work."

One thing I've learned, going along with what my single-mom friend had to offer, is that if I do make a decision after doing the homework, and perhaps it turns out wrong, I can almost always change it. If I pick out paint for one of our rooms in the house and end up not liking it, so what? I can always change it. That has helped me get unstuck in some of the more daily decisions that have confronted me. Decisions that affect the rest of your life deserve more thought and prayer. But those, too, can be reevaluated with the same thought and prayer down the line. Nothing is *really* permanent . . . except God's love.

LAYERS OF POOR SELF-IMAGE

I've been weighed down by weight issues all my adult life. It's been a constant battle, and I've benefited by learning that the source of this destructive life-layer is the emotional wounding I endured as a child, abused by a trusted babysitter. Yes, understanding helps . . . but it doesn't always keep me away from those comforting chocolate chip cookies! In the midst of whatever diet I'm on at the time (and I'm *always* on a diet, it seems), whenever a hurtful or stressful situation occurs, I find myself wondering what there is to eat.

And knowing that's how I respond to stress, I've discovered another destructive layer that I'm determined to shed: hoarding. I hoard food, time, affection, words of affirmation, sleep. I feel like I'm always "saving up," anticipating hard times ahead when I'll need some comforting.

It's not hoarding in the traditional sense. I don't store up great quantities of food in some secret place. More likely, it's a couple of granola bars or protein snacks I've stuck in my purse "just in case." And somehow, "just in case" always happens. I always end up eating them. What happens is, as I'm heading out of the house bound for the airport or heading out of the hotel bound for the arena, the thought occurs to me, *I might get hungry. I'd better take along something to eat, just in case.*

And remember, for me *might get hungry* can also mean *may get tense* or *may get stressed* or *may get hurt* or *may get . . . who knows what!* In other words, something might happen, like *I might need to breathe or something,* and then I'd need food to survive the attack. And there are all sorts of reasons why a sweet, high-calorie snack bar is better than, say, a bag of baby carrots or a nice, shiny apple. I couldn't exactly sit on "the porch" next to the stage at a Women of Faith conference gnawing on an apple or chomping on carrots, could I? But I could slip a granola bar into my pocket and break off one little bite at a time and—achoo!—discreetly pop it into my mouth during a dainty little cough or sneeze.

And here's another interesting thing I've realized about those protein bars. A lot of them are considered *meal replacements*. We are to eat them *instead* of a meal. More often what happens is that we consider them *snacks* and eat them *in addition to* our regularly scheduled meal. We kid ourselves into thinking we're doing good because we're eating this "healthy" thing instead of candy. But the truth is they may have the same (or higher) calorie count as candy.

When I'm being honest, I go back to that hoarding issue and ask myself, *Just when have you ever been in danger of starving, young lady?* And I remind myself I'm just playing games; whether it's a protein bar or a candy bar, I really don't need either one. I can wait until mealtime and have a big salad instead.

So when I'm feeling strong (and I'm proud to say I do feel stronger every day, thank You, Jesus!), I attack that layer of hoarding. I say, *Sandi, if you put those protein bars in your purse or your pocket, you* will *eat them. And then you'll be mad at yourself, and you'll feel like a miserable failure even though right now you know good and well that you're actually quite an awesome woman made in God's own image. So you just put those snack bars right back in the cabinet (or better yet, the trash can). You'll survive one more day without them. After all, isn't there a Scripture verse that says God will supply all my needs? Uh-huh. There it is, Philippians 4:19: "And my God will meet all your needs according to his glorious riches in Christ Jesus."*

Sometimes I gang up on myself during these little lectures and think, *And just when have you ever been hungry, and absolutely no food was available? Face it, girl, you're*

*never far from food. So let's just move on and leave that
layer—and those protein bars—behind.*

Then, anytime I make it out the door without them, I
smile and tell myself, *You are such a good girl!* And if I
make it through the day without cheating and rewrapping
myself in that layer of comfort food . . . I brush my teeth,
pop into bed, and turn out the light really fast to reinforce
the idea that I'm celebrating my success.

WAITING FOR REAL HUNGER

Here's an interesting revelation I have learned along the way.
I have never—at least I don't remember—ever felt hunger.
It has been my habit to supersede my feeling of hunger by
eating before it's time. This may sound very strange to those
of you who layer yourselves differently. But for my fellow
layered sisters, I know you get what I'm saying.

As I began to address what real hunger feels like, I flashed
back to a time when my oldest daughter, Anna, was a baby,
and I was a brand-new mother. I remembered thinking, *I
am going to be the best mother in the whole entire world. My
child will never have to cry because I will anticipate her each
and every need.* Hel-loooo?! Talk about setting up myself
for failure right from the start. The first time Anna cried, I
was ready to sign up for Bad Moms Anonymous!

I now realize that it's vital for a child to learn to *express*
her needs so she can experience having those needs met.

Sometimes a child needs to cry. For example, if the child is crying because she's hungry, then the child needs to be fed. And when she *is* fed, she learns to trust. She learns that she doesn't have to be *afraid* that she'll go hungry. No, experience teaches her that the world is a good place, where others hear her and care about her. The child won't learn anything at all if she doesn't have the freedom and, yes, the *choice* to say, "Help me. I need something."

Wanting to be the perfect mother—and realizing I'm not—probably has caused me to try to make up for my imperfections ever since. For example, I used to sit at the dinner table with my kids, and when they didn't eat their green beans, I would immediately think, *They're trying to tell me something. Not eating their green beans really means they need* _____. (I'd fill in the blank, depending on what was currently going on in our lives.) At the time, I tended to blame every possible issue on the fact that my children had been through a divorce and were now part of a blended family. I couldn't see through my own layers of worrying about those issues to realize that sometimes things can just be taken at face value. Sometimes when a kid doesn't eat her green beans, it just means she doesn't like green beans!

LEARNING THE WRONG LESSONS

I see now that when my abuse happened, it turned upside down this whole needs/needs-met concept, especially the part about expressing those needs. I learned not to express that I needed to feel safe or that I was feeling scared or angry. I learned the lesson, "Lie there and shut up." So I have been shutting up about my needs and compensating my management of those needs by trying to head them off before they arise. As a result, I've lived much of my life trying to get people to magically see through my layers even though I'm not speaking my mind and saying what I really mean. I think I've been speaking in some kind of code, hoping someone out there would hear and understand what I really need. But how could they?

As I develop my sense of good self-esteem and learn to not constantly second-guess myself, I'm learning to trust my needs (and choices), express them appropriately, and believe that they will be met in a healthy way.

> *I've been speaking in some kind of code, hoping someone out there would hear and understand what I really need.*

For a long time, the way I'd layered myself in extra weight was a huge downer for me, something I was aware of almost all the time. It's still something I struggle with; I'd love to be a size 4 like my friend Carolyn. But more than I want to be smaller, I want to be *healthy* so I can be an active, involved wife, mother, and friend. And the fact is, except for these extra pounds, I'm blessed with good health. So, instead of fretting about my weight, I try hard to focus on feeling good about feeling good.

On my good days, I do my best to eat a healthy, balanced diet, and I simply enjoy being me. I really have come to like and accept *me* from the inside looking out. On my troublesome days, I look in the mirror and groan, unable to see the abundantly blessed person inside a body that is abundantly layered. Then that two-word prayer fills my head and my heart once more: *God, help!*

He answers that plea by reminding me to look in the mirror, not with my own eyes but with *His*.

SEEING THE REAL ME

I met a new friend a few years ago, Jennifer Rothschild. She is a beautiful woman and a gifted speaker and communicator. She is also blind—yet she sees things that I still long to see. She said at a Women of Faith conference that since she couldn't see herself in the earthly mirror, she had to learn to see herself in the mirror of God's love and grace.

Wow! Did that hit home with me. I need to do the same thing.

Jennifer has had to get comfortable with the fact that she is blind. The truth is we all have difficulties or problems or issues or struggles we have to deal with and work through, removing the layers we've piled onto those issues to ease the hurt or buffer the responses those issues cause in others. In her books, Jennifer has revealed how she's overcome many of her layering issues, and as I've gotten to know her, I've learned from her.

It's funny, but I began to realize that one of the reasons I'm so comfortable around Jennifer is, well, she can't *see* me, so it's easy to believe she loves the real me, authentic and unlayered, because she doesn't know what I look like.

While that subconscious thought made me feel especially comfortable around Jennifer, it was actually a sad revelation about my feelings for myself. I want to move through life with the same attitude toward myself that I perceive Jennifer has about me. I want to be so comfortable with myself that whether my weight is up or down, I know with all my heart that I'm God's princess.

And I want to extend Jennifer's same love-filled attitude toward others, no matter what their issue is. I want to have the attitude another friend of mine had when she was in the hospital recently.

After surgery, my friend shared a room for a few hours with another surgical patient she talked to but didn't see. They were separated by a curtain and were groggy from anesthesia, so they didn't try to talk. Besides, the other woman's husband was with her, and my friend—I'll call her Amy—was alone.

She couldn't help but overhear the husband telling his wife, "Honey, you look so pretty, even after what you've been through. Would you like me to brush your hair for you?"

"That would be nice, thank you," the other woman said. "And could you hand me my lipstick?"

The husband spoke so lovingly to his wife, fixing her hair, telling her how pretty she looked. Amy smiled, picturing the stylish couple on the other side of the curtain.

The doctor came in and discharged the other woman, and the husband left to get the car. When it was just the two of them in the room, the other woman said gently, "Hello, over there! I hope we didn't disturb you with all the talking."

"Oh, no," Amy answered, "but I couldn't help notice what a sweet husband you have."

The woman chuckled. "He's a sweetie all right. He treats me like I'm a queen." Then the woman asked Amy what kind of surgery she'd had. "Gall bladder," Amy answered. "How about you?"

Just then the woman's cell phone rang, interrupting their brief conversation. It was her husband, telling her he had the car at the hospital entrance. An attendant instantly appeared with a wheelchair to take the woman to the door. The woman asked the attendant to push her past the curtain so she could say good-bye to Amy—who was amazed to see an enormous woman probably weighing four hundred pounds or more.

The woman in the wheelchair said merrily, "Well, wish me luck. I had gastric bypass surgery. I'm hoping to lose two hundred pounds this year!"

The experience was a layering lesson for Amy. When she couldn't see the woman but could only hear her voice and her interaction with her adoring husband, Amy had pictured her as a slim and trim, high-fashion beauty queen.

When she saw the woman's size, she felt her unspoken attitude try to change—and then she quickly reversed it.

"I've thought about it ever since then, realizing how the husband obviously saw through the extra layers on his wife's body to love and appreciate the real woman inside. and how, overhearing his loving remarks, I pictured the woman differently than she actually appeared," Amy said. "It's hard to explain the impact it has had on my thinking, but it has been a very valuable lesson."

THE OPINION THAT MATTERS

I've learned a lot of valuable lessons as I work through my layers. For one, I know without a doubt that God thinks I am wonderful. He thinks you are wonderful too. We share that status with all of creation, including the ancient psalmist, who wrote, "I praise you because I am fearfully and wonderfully made; your works are wonderful, I know that full well" (139:14).

So when I look in the mirror with Sandi's eyes, I may see an overweight woman with a puffy face and droopy flesh. But when I look at my reflection with God's eyes, I recognize myself as one of His works and remember that all His works are wonderful. After all, a mirror is just a reflection; it isn't the real me. So what if I choose—ah, there's that word again—to be a reflection of His grace and His love, instead of—or in addition to—what I see in the mirror? That's where real beauty resides. Deep inside, I know that to be true. Now I want to *live* it as intensely as I *believe* it.

And then there are those other earthly eyes that find me beautiful, and oh, what a blessing they are to me. My husband Don thinks I'm gorgeous; he has told me so many times over the last thirteen years—told me so sweetly and sincerely that I fully believe him. When I'm around him, I *feel* beautiful. My spirit soars, my confidence skyrockets, and all those ugly imaginary layers just seem to melt away.

I used to think he was just saying I'm beautiful to be nice and to be a supportive husband. Then I started thinking, *Wow! He really means it, so God must have given him special eyes to see me.*

Now I'm beginning to believe that not only am I beautiful in his eyes, I am beautiful, period!—in a sassy kind of way. That woman who shared the hospital room with my friend Amy has been blessed with the same kind of husband, one who loves and encourages her for herself, regardless of what the world says about her appearance. What a nurturing and awesome gift that is.

When I'm in that love-layered mode, I can look in the mirror and smile, feeling invincible because I know I've got my priorities straight.

The same thing happens to me but in a different way when I'm with our eight children. I know without a doubt that they think I'm beautiful too. Like Don (and Jesus!), they love me unconditionally, whether I'm the size of a toothpick—or an oak tree. And, sister, that love feels . . . beautiful!

A few years ago I was considering having breast-reduction surgery. While I was talking about it with Don, our young son Sam overheard us. He quietly slipped up to my side and whispered in my ear, "But, Mom, then you won't be *Mommy* anymore." He was trying to say, *You're beautiful just as you are.*

When I'm in that love-layered mode, I can look in the mirror and smile, feeling invincible because I know I've got my priorities straight. The challenge is to keep those love layers intact while shredding the destructive attitudes and shedding the negative images.

My friend Marilyn Meberg tells an interesting story about her own struggles with self-image. Marilyn was an only child, the daughter of a Methodist minister and his wife. She remembers, as a little girl, asking her father, "Daddy, do you think I'm pretty?"

"Honey, you may not be pretty, but you're smart, and that's even more important than being pretty," her father would say.

Through the years, Marilyn, like most of us girls, experimented with various fashions, hairstyles, and makeup. And sometimes, when she thought she'd found a new way to improve her looks, she would ask her father again, "Daddy, do you think I'm pretty *now*?"

But he would always answer the same way: "You're not pretty, Marilyn, but you're very smart, and that's what really matters."

Now, if you've seen Marilyn, maybe during a conference somewhere or pictured on the cover of one of her books, you know she's not only brilliantly smart but also a very attractive woman. In fact, when my business manager and her husband came to one of the Women of Faith conferences, her husband, Adam, leaned over to me and said, "That Marilyn is a hottie." And I agree. Who knows why Marilyn's dad couldn't bring himself to compliment her on her appearance? It might be that she grew up during an era when parents thought it was harmful to flatter their children for fear it would make them vain and conceited later in life. In any case, she never got to hear those words—until near the end of her father's life.

By then Marilyn was a professional mental health therapist with enough experience to know that her value as a human being wasn't dependent on her father's opinion of her looks. But still, she found herself asking him again one day as she sat at his bedside shortly before his death.

Although it feels good to be layered by others' high opinions, in the end, only God's opinion matters.

"Daddy," she said, "you always told me I wasn't pretty, but I was smart, and that was better. Did you really never think I was pretty?"

Her dad smiled and patted her hand. "Yes, sweetheart, you're very pretty. I've always thought you were beautiful," he said.

That night, Marilyn couldn't wait to get home and tell her husband, Ken. "Guess what," she said. "Daddy finally told me he thinks I'm pretty."

Ken pulled her into his arms and kissed her gently. "Ah, honey," he said, "you know he's zoned out on painkillers right now. He doesn't know what he's saying."

Ken was, of course, teasing Marilyn because I knew for a fact that Ken thought Marilyn was a hottie too.

Isn't that a hoot? It makes me laugh—but also makes me realize the power others hold over us sometimes by the opinions they have of us. And although it feels good to be layered by others' high opinions, in the end, only God's opinion matters.

Max Lucado teaches this lesson in his wonderful children's book *You Are Special*. It's a story about little wooden people called Wemmicks who were made by a wood-carver named Eli. The Wemmicks expressed their opinions of each other by plastering each other with stickers shaped like stars and dots. If they thought someone looked good or acted properly, they gave that Wemmick a star. But the Wemmicks who weren't quite perfect or who made mistakes got dots.

Punchinello was an accident-prone Wemmick who found himself layered with dots, and those dots made him sad. One day he noticed a Wemmick, Lucia, who didn't have *any* dots. It turned out that the other Wemmicks' stickers wouldn't stick to Lucia. Whenever they tried to put a star or a dot on her, it fell right off. When Punchinello asked Lucia about it, she sent him to see Eli, the wood-carver.

Eli told Punchinello that the stickers didn't stick to Lucia "because she has decided that what I think is more important than what others think . . . The more you trust my love, the less you care about their stickers."[1]

ANOTHER LOOK IN THE MIRROR

I think of Punchinello as I make myself stand in front of the mirror again. Just as his maker's words made Punchinello feel better about himself, so do my Maker's words make me feel better about myself. Sure, I value the positive opinions my husband and my children have about my looks. But beneath all the layers, at the core of my being, the opinion that really matters is God's.

The question is, will I choose to receive what God says about me? After all, it's not what *they* think of me that counts; it's *His* love and strength that perfect me. First John 4:12 says, "If we love one another, God dwells deeply within us, and his love becomes complete in us— perfect love!" (MSG). And 2 Samuel 22:33 reminds us, "It is God who arms me with strength and makes my way perfect." When I set my mind on Him, he makes me "completely whole" (Isaiah 26:3 MSG).

It's not what they think of me that counts; it's His love and strength that perfect me.

And the truth is, often people will see the person I am

choosing to reflect. So if I move through this life feeling unloved, fat, unhealthy, stupid, or whatever, that is how people are going to unconsciously see me. But when I truly choose to reflect the beautiful-and-beloved-princess attitude, people unconsciously see me that way as well. I have a lot to do with how others see me—and not just what I do to myself (good or bad) physically, but also mentally. Proverbs 23:7 reminds us that what we think, we become.

So what do I need now?

I need to memorize Psalm 118:23 and repeat it to myself each time I look in the mirror: "This is GOD's work. We rub our eyes—we can hardly believe it!" (MSG)

So what do you need now?

I need _____

_____

_____

3

*Replacing Guilt with Grace
and Coming to Peace with Yourself*

We all arrive at your doorstep sooner or later, loaded with guilt.

—PSALM 65:2 MSG

Sometimes when I'm out on the concourse of a Women of Faith conference, I look up at the line of women waiting to talk to me or to get my autograph, and I feel totally guilt-ridden and incredulous, amazed that anyone would spend even one precious minute of her life waiting on *me*. All those years ago, when I'd made such a huge mess of my life, it was hard to imagine that anyone outside my closest friends and family would ever want to have anything to do with me again.

And yet they come, and I'm humbled and amazed that they do. Amazed because one might say, "I want to lose a hundred pounds so I can be like you." Humbled because some say, "Oh, I just love that song you sang. It really touched my heart." Some just want a CD autographed.

But then I look up and there stands a woman in tears, and I sense what she's going to say.

"Sandi, you know that book you wrote, *Broken on the Back Row*? Well, that's where I am right now," she'll say. "I'm broken on the back row, too, because I've made such a mess of my life."

It takes a lot of courage to wait in line so you can let a stranger peek through your layers of guilt and shame to share something so personal. But broken people like us do it so we can reassure each other, "You're not the only one. You're not alone."

You can't fix broken people with a hammer when what they need is a kind touch and tenderness.

Usually I only have a few seconds at that point, but my goal is to make sure that hurting woman feels heard and understood. I want her to know she's taken an important first step; she's shared her dark secret. That's not the time to suddenly start spouting Scripture verses, such as "Greater is he who is in you than he who is in the world." That can come later when she feels strong enough to work through her guilt with her God and her family and her church. At that point, I just want to hold her and say, "I understand."

You can't fix broken people with a hammer when what they need is a kind touch and tenderness. And here's the important thing: shedding those dark, hurtful layers and beginning the healing process starts with *them*. It has to be their choice. And it often starts, I've learned, when they are willing to be a little vulnerable because I've been vulnerable, too, by sharing the worst things about myself . . . or so that's what they tell me in the signing line.

CONSEQUENCES AND GUILT

A lot of ugly things happened to me because of my sinful actions all those years ago. I was at the peak of my musical career, and suddenly churches and other venues canceled concerts. Radio stations refused to play my music. Record deals were kicked to the back burner. All of those consequences were hard and hurtful. But none of them were as agonizing as knowing I had hindered the work of God's kingdom and hurt the hearts of my children.

Sometimes I hear friends talk about feeling guilty because they did something that was a little less than honest. Maybe they substituted sweetener for sugar in the apple pie even though they know their overweight husbands think sweetener should be banned—or at least categorized as a controlled substance. Maybe they spent some of the grocery money on a pedicure or called in sick to Bible study then slipped off for coffee with a friend. Maybe they lied about going out of town this weekend so they wouldn't have to babysit their sister's kids. Most of us have layered on some guilt now and then when being totally honest is a little inconvenient or a little uncomfortable, and we believe no actual harm was done.

But my case was different. I suppose we all feel that way when we make mistakes. But I didn't just *feel* guilty. I *was* guilty! During my separation and divorce, and my falling in love with Don in between the two, I seemed to bounce from one miserable low point to another. And each time I landed, I pulled on another cushioning layer of guilt and shame, trying to ease the pain when what I really needed was to drag the tattered layers of my life to the foot of the cross—and leave them there.

Eventually I was so insulated by all the worthless coverings of guilt-induced misery that I became disconnected from the things I needed most: God's gracious love and forgiveness. Although I'd been brought up in the church and could recite countless verses about salvation backward and forward, somehow I just couldn't believe His grace was powerful enough to cover the awful sin I'd committed. So I remained hidden behind layer upon layer of guilt and shame—so many layers that the grace I needed and insisted I still believed in just couldn't find its way through to me.

> *I seemed to bounce from one miserable low point to another. And each time I landed, I pulled on another cushioning layer of guilt and shame.*

When I first met Sheila Walsh some twenty years ago, there was something truly honest and real in her that drew me to her (not to mention her wonderful Scottish brogue). I remember hearing her speak a few years after she, too, had gone through some deep and personal struggles and being mesmerized by what she was saying, sharing openly about her own time in the psyche ward of a hospital.

I particularly related to one story she told about *craft time* in the hospital. She and the other patients were given a handful of clay and directed to "sculpt" their feelings and how they viewed themselves. Sheila said it felt like a stupid exercise, almost demeaning, as though she and the other patients were in kindergarten.

But then, recalled Sheila, the strangest thing happened. Without her realizing it, her hands began to fashion that clay into something that astonished her. As she looked down at her "creation," she saw that she had formed a fortress wall—high and impenetrable. And inside that huge wall was a small lonely figure with arms long enough to reach over the walls to comfort others, but the walls were too high for anyone to reach her. Somehow she knew that she was that little lump of clay. She saw that she had created a model of how she had literally walled herself away from life, shielding herself from life's hurts with layer upon layer of hardened protection.

With God's help, and the help of mental health professionals, she started peeling back the hardened layers of that walled fortress, allowing herself to be embraced instead by God's powerful love and healing grace.

FOUND BY GOD

In the midst of that agonizing time, I decided to visit a new church in Anderson, Indiana, where I've lived now for nearly thirty years. What happened to me there became the basis for my book *Broken on the Back Row*. I'll spare you the details here and just say that the Sunday service was so crowded, I ended up on the back row of the balcony, right under the big stained-glass window. And almost as soon as I sat down, I started crying. Everything just seemed to come crashing down on me, and I quietly cried through the entire hour-long service, crushed and overwhelmed by the devastating havoc I had created in my life and my children's.

Then right before the invitation hymn, the pastor, Jim Lyon, stepped off the platform and spoke right to me. Oh, he didn't *know* he was talking to me. He couldn't even see me bawling my eyes out up there in the rafters. He thought he was just extending the same kind of broad, warm invitation he shares at every service. He simply said what God put on his heart that day without knowing God was speaking directly to me. "If you're visiting with us today, we're glad you're here, and we'd like to get to know you," he said.

Oh no, you wouldn't, I thought. *Not if you knew what I have done.*

Then Pastor Lyon (and God) continued. "But if you're visiting us this morning, and you don't want to tell us your name, that's okay. If all you want to do is sit on the back row of the balcony and cry, that's okay too."

My head popped up, and my tear-filled eyes widened.

"We serve a God who knows how to find you," Pastor Lyon continued. "He hasn't forgotten you. He's the God of second chances and new beginnings."

Even now, after I've told and written about that day so many times, it still takes my breath away. And let me just suggest that while you're letting this powerful scene soak into your brain, think back to chapter 2 when I described that little God moment about the dieting dilemma. Now let me ask you something: if *you* had been sitting on the back row of the balcony that day, crying your eyes out, and you'd heard those amazing words spoken right into your heart by someone you'd never met . . . would *you* be surprised fifteen years later if the doorbell rang as soon as you'd thrown up that little "God, help!" prayer about choosing the right diet?

What I've now proved through my own personal experience is what Pastor Lyon was saying that Sunday morning in church: God knows where you are. He will find you no matter how far you've fallen, no matter how far up in the balcony you try to hide, no matter how many layers you try to put between you and God. Wherever you are, whatever you've done, if you'll let Him, God will wrap you in His amazing grace that vaporizes all the sins you've committed, no matter how

No matter what kind of mess you've made . . . if you ask Him to, He will forgive you and give you another chance.

many layers you've piled on to keep from exposing your mistakes.

And here's the best part: no matter what kind of mess you've made, whether it's simply stupid or horribly destructive, if you ask Him to, He will forgive you and give you another chance to live your earthly life for Him—and your eternal life *with* Him.

Girlfriend, it just doesn't get any better than that!

HEALED BY LOVE, SAVED BY GRACE

When I discussed my idea for this book with my friend Mary Graham, who's also the president of Women of Faith, she sent me an e-mail that described a tangible analogy of the emotional layers I'm writing about.

"When I was a little girl," she said, "the walls in our very old frame house were covered in wallpaper. Every few years when the wallpaper got dirty, new wallpaper covered the old. If you were a little girl and you found a little hole and picked at it long enough, you could find as many different wallpapers as you had the patience to reveal. (Of course, a little girl could also get in trouble for doing this. Don't ask me how I know.) Peeling off the layers was fascinating to me and revealed the history of the room. In the same way, we 'paper' our pain in ways that make sense to us individually rather than risk exposing it. Layer upon layer, we hide, and grace can't make its way to us to cover our guilt and shame."

Mary's wise and insightful wallpaper analogy prompted corollaries in my own mind, especially my laborious attempts at home-decorating makeovers. Picking at a little hole in the wallpaper is one thing, but if you've ever tried to strip the wallpaper from a whole room, you know that, overall, that stuff can really be stuck on there! Sometimes it takes days of hard, determined work to strip the walls bare.

The emotional and behavioral layers of guilt and shame that we pull over ourselves, trying to cover our sin, can be equally difficult to remove. Sure, we may find little holes here and there and may get a glimpse of our true selves, but overall, it takes work to strip away the layers so God's grace can do its best work.

Not that God makes it difficult. All *He* requires of us is that we ask His forgiveness—and believe that His Son's death and resurrection makes that forgiveness possible . . .

Layer upon layer, we hide, and grace can't make its way to us to cover our guilt and shame.

even when we ask for it again and again. Luci Swindoll says that her brother Chuck Swindoll once told her the secret is to "just show up." We just show up and let God do the rest.

First John 2:12 says, "I remind you, my dear children: Your sins are forgiven in Jesus' name" (MSG). And Acts 2:38 quotes the apostle Peter's straightforward directions for how to "change your life. Turn to God and be baptized,

each of you, in the name of Jesus Christ, so your sins are
forgiven. Receive the gift of the Holy Spirit" (MSG).

No, God made salvation simple and grace readily available. It is we humans who somehow feel the need to layer
His plan with cultural complications. I felt that need when
I talked with Pastor Lyon later and said I hoped to become
a regular attendee. (In my denomination, we don't call
ourselves "members" or "parishioners.") In a process that
continued over several years, I laid out the sordid details
of my failed marriage and the scandalous affair, and shared
my hope that the church would bless my plans to eventually be married again—to Don.

He reminded me that all *God* required was that I con-
fess my sin, repent of it, and ask His forgiveness. Once
that was done, my guilt was washed away by Jesus' blood
on the cross and God's promises of grace.

But Pastor Lyon also understood my need to do something
more so that I felt fully restored to the church congregation.
We set up a schedule of procedures and meetings with church
leaders that helped Don and me work through that process of
restoration. Basically, what happened in those meetings was
that the layers of old, dirty "wallpaper" were peeled away
from my life, and the real me was exposed.

It may sound silly, but when I think of Mary's wallpaper analogy and the long process I went through to feel
restored, I picture those old, hurtful layers being ripped
away, and then I see myself being painted with the super-
sticky love of those elders and *wallpapered* directly to the

heart of God. Now I know *nothing* will ever peel me off of Him! I'm one of His children (and so are you), and He has promised He's "sticking with [us], not leaving [us] for a minute" (Isaiah 42:16 MSG).

RESCUED FROM THE BACK ROW

At the end of the nearly two-year period of restoration (and the beginning of a wonderful new experience in the church), Don and I stood in front of that congregation as the subject of Pastor's Lyon's sermon one Sunday. He described the steps we'd taken to become whole again. He invited anyone who felt uncomfortable with our situation to make arrangements to speak with us directly. But that turned out to be unnecessary.

That day—and every time I had occasion to stand in front of my church after that—I couldn't help but glance up to the balcony and remember how God found me there. With the light pouring in through the huge stained-glass window, the people sitting up there were backlit. It was hard to see their faces. But standing there in the front of the church, I never failed to pray, *Lord, if there's someone up there whose heart is broken and whose life is in turmoil, help her feel the same hope I felt that day You rescued me from the back row of the balcony.*

It has happened dozens of times. The last time was during my daughter Anna's wedding to Collin, the young man Don and I now consider our ninth child. During the ceremony, one of the bridesmaids—Don's daughter, Mollie—probably overcome by the excitement of the day, became light-headed and sank to the floor. Without a moment's pause, everyone in Anna's big, once-broken family sprang into action as a team: spouses, ex-spouses, siblings, and step-siblings fanning, patting, fetching water, cooing, and encouraging the stricken loved one.

Even then, during all the hubbub, as I sat next to Mollie on the front row and held her hand while she caught her breath and prepared to resume her position . . . even then, I couldn't help but glance up at the church balcony again and marvel at the miracle God had worked in my life. Once, in the same place where I had sat alone on the back row and wept, I now sat down front, surrounded by my wonderfully enlarged family, my new and awesome church, and my devoted circle of friends.

I couldn't help but glance up to the balcony and remember how God found me there.

Thank You, God! I prayed.

Our congregation moved into a new building not too long ago. The old back row of the balcony is a thing of the past. No matter. God moved into our new building with us. Amazingly, He hangs out in your church, too, *and* in your home. There may not be a physical balcony there, but you may be sitting on the back row of an emotional balcony, feeling lost and layered with guilt and shame. I understand. Been there, done that. And ever since then, it's been my great joy to find others there and share my story with them. I tell how God found me right where they are now, and I let them know He can find them, too, wherever and whatever they're hiding.

REACHING OUT TO
THOSE BACK-ROW GALS

My longing to help other back-row gals reminds me of a story about Barbara Johnson, one of the founding speakers of Women of Faith. Barbara had a wonderful way of reaching out to us broken gals on the back row of the balcony, both emotionally—and literally. She always said that God had blessed her with a "bubble of joy" even though she had endured a lot of heartache in her life, including the death of two sons and the alienation of a third son after she learned he was homosexual. She spent the last half of her life helping other hurting parents learn to laugh again when their hearts were broken.

For many years, until she was incapacitated by a brain tumor in 2001, Barbara spoke all over the country at Christian conferences, including Women of Faith events in huge arenas. Sally, one of the helpers who traveled with Barbara, was often given a task that she found both rewarding and terrifying. Somehow, Sally said, Barbara always ended up with some extra VIP tickets for the arena conferences. And just as Barbara was heading for the platform at the start of the conference, she would point at some dark corner of the arena, up near the ceiling, hand Sally those extra tickets, and say, "You know what to do."

What Barb wanted Sally to do was find the women with the worst seats in the house and bring them down to those VIP seats on the front row.

This would have been a pleasure for Sally to do, except that she was afraid of heights. And the worst seats in the house—in arenas big enough to hold sometimes twenty-five thousand women—were always on the tippy-top row of the highest level of seats.

In other words, the back row of the balcony.

Sally would draw in a deep breath, take a gulp of water, and head upward. Sometimes she had to go up two long escalators or ride the elevator up several floors to get to the top level of the arena. Then she would walk from the concourse through the little tunnel and out to the landing with her eyes glued to the floor because she was afraid to look over the guardrail and see just how high up she was.

Find the women with the worst seats in the house and bring them down to those VIP seats on the front row.

With both hands on the handrail —when she was lucky enough to be in an arena that *had* handrails—she would start climbing the steps up to the top row. If there wasn't a handrail, she said, she sometimes would be stooped over with her hands touching the steps in front of her, trying desperately to keep her balance—and her breakfast.

Meanwhile, the women seated in the top row would be watching this strange woman, huffing and puffing, stooped over and obviously in distress, climbing ever closer toward them. When Sally finally reached the worst seats in the house, it usually took her several minutes to catch her breath so that she could finally speak. By then the women were convinced Sally was beset with mental problems.

"Hi," she would wheeze. "Barbara Johnson sent me up here to get you." Then came the part that was the real mixed blessing for Sally. She would force herself to look down at the floor of the arena, far below, to the empty seats right in front of the platform. "See that row of empty chairs down there? See? Under the stage lights? Those empty seats on the front row? Barb wants me to take you down there so you can sit in those good seats instead of up here in the rafters."

The women's reaction was almost always the same. "Really?" they would say. "Barbara Johnson sent you to get *us*? Oh, that's so nice of her. But . . . why would she do that?"

Sally would smile and shrug. "That's just Barbara," she would say. "She says she's blessed to be a blessing."

If you'll let Him, God will find you in the worst place you can imagine. He'll climb up the steep steps, blow away your layers of guilt and shame, and move you right down to the front row of His love.

Oh, and there's just one more thing you need to remember. Sometimes God comes to you disguised as someone else . . . say, a middle-aged, scared-of-heights woman named

Sally, or a blonde-haired, mother-of-many singer named Sandi. It may take us a while to work our way up the steps of your balcony or through your layers to get to you. But when we finally arrive, out of breath and full of joy, you'll know God found you up there. And He sent us to get you.

So what do I need now?

I need to go to the Lord's Psalm 51 Laundromat: "Generous in love—God, give grace! Huge in mercy—wipe out my bad record. Scrub away my guilt, soak out my sins in your laundry" (vv. 1–2 MSG).

So what do you need now?

I need _____

_____

_____

_____

4

Reclaiming God's Perfectly Imperfect Creation: Me!

*Unlike the culture around you, always dragging you down
to its level of immaturity, God brings the best out of you.*

—ROMANS 12:2 MSG

S am asked today what I was doing. He'd noticed that
I've been working a lot more than usual on my com-
puter lately. I told him I was working on a new book.
He asked what the title was, and I told him it was called
Layers.

He said, "Oh, is it about onions?"

Don't you love the unpretentious wisdom of children? I
told Sam, "Well, I really hadn't planned to include onions,
but now that I think of it . . . they're a good illustration of
what I'm trying to say." As you peel back the dried-up layers on the outside of the onion, you can get to the heart of
the flavor inside. That's what I'm learning to do as I peel
off the unnecessary habits and unhealthy emotions and

attitudes that keep me from enjoying and sharing the true flavor of my heart.

One of the layers I hope to peel away is my negative attitude about my appearance. By now it's probably no surprise to you that I tend to have body-image problems. I hate the fact that I struggle constantly with my weight. And here we are, almost halfway through the book, and maybe you're wondering when the tone is going to change to the one we hear in those commercials: "I did it! I'm a size 4 now, and this diet is *so* easy and *so* much fun. You'll love it. And before you know it, you'll be a size 4 too."

Sorry, girlfriends. It ain't happenin'.

Oh, sure, I'm plugging away at it, and I've lost some pounds. But if I were doing a commercial right now, I'd probably say, "Dieting stinks! I hate it. I've tried ten gazillion diets and spent *years* trying to lose weight. And now look at me. I'm still a size none-of-your-business."

I try to be a good Christian and live my life as close as I can to the way Jesus showed me how to live it. I believe everything God tells me in the Bible. Honestly, I do. I believe He created me and cherishes me. Like many of you, I can quote by heart those powerful words in the Psalms: "For you created my inmost being; you knit me together in my mother's womb. I praise you because I am fearfully and wonderfully made; your works are wonderful, I know that full well" (139:13–14).

And yet one of the hardest things I've had to do over the years is remind myself of those very personal scriptural facts.

Here's how bad it is (or I hope *was*). Every time I record

a new album or write a new book or prepare for a tour or some other similar commitment, I have to have professional photographs taken. I dread those photo sessions more than I dread root canals. In the past, I've hated having my picture taken . . . because I've hated the way I look.

Okay, so there it is: the cold, hard truth. And now just let me take a little break to send up an urgent prayer to my Creator: *I'm sorry, Father. I know in my heart that I am wonderfully made. I know in my heart that You made me the way You want me to be. Forgive me for doubting You. In fact, it's not that I doubt You. I just think I've messed up the body You intended me to have. You probably made me to be a size 4, right? But these hard things happened to me, and I turned to food instead of to You, and now I've covered up that cute size 4 body with all these layers . . .*

When I'm with Don, knowing he adores me and thinks I'm prettier than Miss America and Miss Universe combined, I stand taller (which, of course, makes me look thinner).

I really try not to have that attitude, and much of the time, I succeed. When I'm with Don, knowing he adores me and thinks I'm prettier than Miss America and Miss Universe combined, I stand taller (which, of course, makes me look thinner). I try my best to carry those feelings with me, mentally picturing Don walking on one side of me and Jesus on the other, and their faces are beaming as if they want to tell the world, *She's mine! Isn't she gorgeous?*

That's what I *try* to do. But sometimes that attitude gets covered up by all those old, ugly layers. Something upsets me, and I reach for the cookies. Choices arise, or get taken away, and I get stuck and can't seem to do anything but eat. I know I'm more vulnerable to these feelings when I'm tired or cranky or under stress, so I'm working hard to sense when these situations are coming and prepare myself ahead of time. I pray, *God, help!* And then I listen for the doorbell to ring . . .

I *know* He can help me through these layers, if I'll just ask Him to. And I *know* He sends His angels to shower me with love and encouragement. And every time it happens, I hold on to that moment, determined to remember it when the next challenge comes.

THE TRUTH IS IN THE PROOFS

One of those challenges came last fall when a photo shoot for the cover of my new album was scheduled. Days before the appointment, I felt the dark clouds gathering. I chewed my hangnails, tapped my toes, snapped at family and friends. Finally, during a Women of Faith conference, one of my friends, professional therapist Pat Wenger, asked me if something was wrong.

"I've got a photo shoot coming up, and I always get a knot in my stomach, dreading it so much," I told Pat.

She knows my story, knows my weaknesses and strengths,

and she talked to me about why I felt the way I did. "What happens after the photo session?" she asked. "What happens when you see the proofs?"

"I've never seen them," I said. "Never."

"You've *never* seen them? Don't they send them to you?" Pat asked.

"Oh sure, they send them," I told her. "But I can't stand to look at them. I usually cut them up with scissors and just tell someone else to pick the best one."

"Sandi, you're such a pretty woman," Pat said, shaking her head and reaching for my book *Falling Forward*, which happened to be lying on the table where we sat. Pat looked at the cover. "This is a beautiful picture of you," she said.

"But it's *so* air-brushed!" I argued. "That's not me. It's not me at all. The real me is puffy and blemished. There's always a piece of hair that's sticking out of place. I might as well have a big wart on my nose like some ugly old witch. The real me doesn't look anything like the me in that picture. I look at it and feel like such a fake."

The real me doesn't look anything like the me in that picture.

"Oh, honey!" she said.

Then Pat, being Pat, did more than just coo over me. She used her professional training to help me sort through the issues and contradictions that were layering me with dread about the pictures.

Still, as each day passed, I felt the old knot forming in my stomach.

"You have a *choice*," Pat told me one day, knowing how choice is an emotional issue for me. "What are you going to *choose* to do?"

"I'm going to choose to go to that photo session *and . . .*" It was hard to believe I could even say the words. "I'm going to enjoy it."

Bless her heart; Pat went with me to the photo shoot. Throughout the session, she kept me laughing and focused on seeing myself, not through the photographer's lens but through the eyes of those who love me. She would say, "Think of your sweet husband and family who adore you."

Pat helped me realize there was so much more to focus on besides myself. Photo shoots are just one little stop in my life's journey that over all is blessed with tremendous joy. Even though I would still like fewer physical layers on my body, it isn't the end of the world. It's just part of the journey.

With Pat's help, I got through the photo session without plunging into a week of despair. In fact, after it was all over, I started thinking that it had actually been kind of fun.

But the hardest thing still lay ahead: step two would be looking at the proofs a couple of weeks later. I'll tell you later how that went . . .

REMEMBER THE INNOCENT FIVE-YEAR-OLD

Thinking about the hard time I've had getting through past photo sessions launched me into a whole new area of self-discovery. With Pat's help, I started thinking about how I've *always* disliked seeing pictures of myself, even when I was younger and a few layers lighter. I know a lot of people say they share my dislike—but how many have a chronic scissors habit as I do? Thinking about it, I started flipping through some photo books, looking at pictures of my family and me as I was growing up.

There are the pictures of me with all of them as we enjoyed summer musical tours as the Ron Patty Family: Mom and Dad with my brothers, Mike and Craig, and me during our adolescent and teenage years. I look at the pictures and squirm a bit. I just flat-out don't like looking at those images. Those were happy times, no doubt about it, but when I look at those pictures of young Sandi, there's something there that bothers me. I look at her and see the emotional layers already in place. *She's got a secret. She doesn't understand it, but it makes her feel dirty and ashamed,* I think, looking at her.

I see it even when I look at the photo of myself as a smiling, blonde-haired, blue-eyed California teenager standing outside in our driveway, wearing my cheerleader outfit, posed with knees bent, one arm up, one arm out, obviously in the middle of a favorite cheer.

I kept going back through the pictures, watching myself magically appear younger and younger until I came to a picture of myself in second grade when I would have been about seven. And gradually the truth became clear to me: *The Sandi in all these pictures still thought the abuse was her fault. She thought she'd done something very bad to have caused it, and she desperately wanted to keep that "something" a secret. But she didn't know what it was. So she pulled on protective layers of guilt and shame and other false beliefs to keep her secret hidden.*

About the time I was going through this process of self-discovery (or maybe I should say self-*re*discovery), a couple of other things happened that helped me sort through all these feelings. First, I had a strange dream.

It's too bizarre and convoluted to share in total, but thinking about it later brought a few more things into perspective for me.

The Sandi in all these pictures still thought the abuse was her fault.

In the dream, I was at a Women of Faith conference, and several gospel choirs, including both men and women, were performing. Suddenly someone in one of the choirs shouted out something rather disturbing. He was expressing his honest feelings about a specific group of people, shouting it out in a setting where it was totally inappropriate. (It's also inappropriate for this book!) Everyone else gasped, and the arena immediately grew quiet. Then I stood up and did a "slow clap," publicly applauding the man. "Well, good for you!" I proclaimed. "We can't get anywhere if we're not honest about our feelings."

Then other people in my dream began to clap, supporting my shocking agreement with the man's statement. But instead of being encouraged, I began to cry. Then I felt everyone's hands on me, the way we place our hands on each other as we pray together before the conference begins. Feeling my friends' love flowing through their hands made me feel so safe, so secure. Someone hurriedly brought Lana Bateman out from backstage. (Lana travels everywhere with Women of Faith as our prayer intercessor. She's also one of the people who helped me when I first felt ready to talk about the baby-sitter's abuse, all those years after it happened. It was Lana who connected me with the professional counselors who've done so much to help me find healing.)

In my dream, Lana gently pushed through the crowd and said softly into my ear, "Lean into it, honey, and feel it *deep*."

She was encouraging me to express my honest feelings. She knew I didn't share the same ugly feelings as the man who had shouted out. But she was commending me for recognizing that someone was willing to be honest in front of others.

Then came the humorous part of the dream. Ever the performer, I suddenly popped out from under the circle of concerned, loving friends and asked, "How much time do I have before I have to go on?"

"Five minutes," someone answered.

"Oh, good," I said. "I've got time to lean into it some more."

Dreams have such a way of melding laughs with lessons, don't they? Patsy Clairmont was the speaker onstage as I was having my little moment of dreamland drama. Despite all the friends hovering around me, I could hear what she was saying. She was talking about a happy memory of dancing alone for the sheer joy of living. As she was speaking, an image popped into my head. It was the memory of five-year-old Sandi, alone in her bedroom, happily dancing and singing her heart out to the music coming from a little record player.

Music was very important in my family. It was more than the source of our family income, it was something we all truly enjoyed. Mom especially nurtured that love in me. When I was a youngster, maybe three or four, she bought me a little record player of my very own.

That was during the age when more and more families were buying complicated stereo and hi-fi systems to play music, and of course those expensive components were off-limits to children. Mom wanted me to be able to enjoy my own music whenever I wanted to without being told, "No! Don't touch!" The result was a little metal record player she bought somewhere, along with a bunch of 45 rpm records— probably nursery rhymes or other children's story songs. She showed me how it worked and turned me loose with it.

I spent hours on end alone in my bedroom, playing those

records, singing along with the music, dancing, and delivering breathtaking performances to imaginary audiences. To be honest, I have only a few specific memories of those musical sessions; I was so young, I just don't remember much more than the happy feelings associated with those times. But I've heard Mom talk about what a beloved thing my first little record player was and how, in my preschool years, I favored it above all other toys.

That's the image from the dream that flashed through my mind when Patsy talked about her own happy memories of dancing alone in her younger days. And in that same instant, I saw something else about little Sandi at age five, something in the innocence twinkling in her eyes.

That was the last time she felt pure, I thought. Then I sensed God's voice gently say to me in my dream, *That's right, honey, and that's who we're going to find.*

GRIEVING LOSSES
WHILE CELEBRATING TRUTH

As you might imagine, I was completely worn out by that long, emotional roller-coaster of a dream! But I also thanked God for it because it gave me additional insights into these feelings that have puzzled and controlled me for so long.

Remembering that sweet little five-year-old playing records in her bedroom, I grieved for her, knowing the hurt that was coming her way, the innocence she was about to lose.

I pictured her flitting around her little record player, playing her music and pretending to be a sugarplum fairy or Little Red Riding Hood, and I realized that in all my efforts to redeem six-year-old Sandi from the effects of the abuse she had received, I had completely forgotten about the precious five-year-old girl before the abuse occurred.

Now I look at her picture and pray, *Thank You, God, for that little girl. Thank You for helping me remember her and reclaim her sweet innocence, her blind trust, and her adoring love for You and her family. I want to be that kind of open, authentic girl again, the girl You created me to be.*

I've learned to like myself again from the inside out. I'm still working on the part about liking myself from the outside in.

I understand that I can't turn back the clock forty years, and of course, there *are* drawbacks to childish innocence. What I'm talking about are the feelings that little girl dancing around the record player had about herself. Five-year-old Sandi was talented—and felt confident about it. She had been making brief appearances since she was little more than two years old when her parents performed in churches. When she started first grade, she tested near the top of her class.

She liked what she saw when she looked in the mirror, and when audiences applauded for her, she honestly appreciated their attention. She may not have remembered to say it as often as she should have, but her most frequent prayer to her Creator back then probably wouldn't have been *God, help!* as it is now, but *Thank You, Jesus!* instead.

That's what I want back. And with God's help, I'm getting there. I've learned to like myself again from the inside out. I'm still working on the part about liking myself from the outside in.

So what do I need now?

I need to look at that woman in the pictures through God's eyes and tell her, "Sugar, I just love how you turned out!" And I'm memorizing this Scripture verse to remind myself of how it happens and who's behind it: "He who began a good work in you will carry it on to completion" (Philippians 1:6).

So what do you need now?

I need _____

_____

_____

5

Healing Hurts

Oh LORD my God, I called to you for help and you healed me.

—PSALM 30:2

Several years ago a friend of mine had a simple little hangnail, no big deal. But he picked at it and bit it and tore it, and instead of going away as most hangnails do, it seemed to grow worse every day. He finally went to the doctor, who diagnosed a severe staph infection.

First the doctor gave my friend some powerful oral and topical antibiotics and instructed him to soak his thumb several times a day in antiseptic wash. Still, the infection grew worse. Concerned, his doctor ordered an X-ray, which revealed that the infection had traveled deeper into his thumb and was dangerously near the bone. The doctor referred him to a surgeon.

Every day for the next two weeks or so, my friend had to go in and let the surgeon peel away layer after layer of dead skin to get to the root of the infection so it could be treated at the source. It was a very painful process, my friend assured me, and he didn't look forward to those appointments. Yet without the diligence of those hurtful daily peelings, the infection could have moved into the bone, perhaps necessitating amputation, or it could have even entered his bloodstream and eventually killed him.

My friend's experience not only illustrates how deeply buried our hidden feelings can be, it also shows how something ridiculously minor and, at first, inconsequential can become a life-threatening danger! When a problem, large or small, eats away at our God-given confidence and our belief that we are God's princesses, we layer ourselves with destructive layers to ease the pain. Soon we've wrapped our lives in a major situation that can be long, slow, and painful to resolve.

And even when we've peeled back the guilt, shame, selfishness, addiction, jealousy—whatever it is we've put between ourselves and a wholesome relationship with God—the healing continues. My friend had to continue to go back to the doctor for about a month after the last peeling treatment, even after the root of the infection had been eliminated, so the doctor could monitor the infected site and make sure that no more staph germs gained a foothold (or maybe a thumbhold?).

I see another illustration when I think about my friend's infection. There were probably faster ways to bring about "healing." The doctor could have just amputated the thumb right from the beginning, but obviously that wasn't the best choice—for several reasons. First, they would never have determined specifically what the source of the infection was. They might have amputated his thumb and later realized the infection's original source was in his toe. Second, my friend would have been permanently disabled without a thumb.

The best option for healing was the one that took the most time. And even though it was also a painful option, it was ultimately the one that brought about complete healing. It's the same with us as we seek help with removing the layers that shield us from the life God intends for us to have.

DOUBLE-SIDED LAYERS

Here's what I hate about dealing with these emotional layers. I think I've eliminated one layer because I do a little work, and I feel better. I pronounce myself healed and convince myself everything's fine. But if I haven't worked down to the root of the problem, it's not really gone. And before I know it, that layer is back in place, and I'm back where I started, separated from God's best.

Earlier we talked about how layers sometimes start out as protective. When we head out into the cold, we talk about wearing layers, both because they trap in more body heat and they give us some flexibility. If we're playing in the snow with the kids, building forts for snowball fights and falling like gingerbread men to make snow angels, and we get overheated, layers let us take off *some* of our warm protection without removing all of it.

Layers can be good. But they can also become toxic because they can hide the infection that's hurting us. We have to dig out the root of that hurt, and to do that, we've got to peel off the layers and let God's healing work within us.

Lately, God's been healing a lot of hurts in my life, but it has taken time, and some of it has been painful. As enlightenment has come, I've realized that I've encased my heart—and literally, my body— with all sorts of layers, emotional and physical, that at first may have been protective but soon became imprisoning.

I have learned that when someone is sexually abused as a child, the layers begin then and there. I was "selected" for abuse because I had the specific looks that triggered that vicious response in my abuser. I layered on not only an attitude of disgust about my appearance but also a subconscious effort to punish my appearance and change it.

Layers can be good. But they can also become toxic because they can hide the infection that's hurting us.

For years I subconsciously thought, *I'm never going to look pleasing again because when you have an attractive look, bad things happen to you.* At the same time, I was caught up in the pervasive culture that surrounds girls and women and says looking good is everything. So I was constantly torn by an inner struggle. And I was chowing down on those cookies and mashed potatoes!

WORKING TO ACHIEVE HEALING

This knowledge came as I worked, *really* worked, to achieve healing with the help of talented counselors, focused prayer, a godly church, and loving family and friends. And even now after all the whole, long process, I know I'm not accurately expressing the situation so that it makes sense to most adults unless they, too, suffered some kind of devastating childhood incident. But it wasn't an adult mind that first began making those unhealthy choices, who vowed never to look attractive again. It was a six-year-old.

Despite the childish naiveté of those vows, they can be very powerful, even more than we can imagine. After enduring a childhood hurt or some kind of abuse, we might vow, "I'll never be hurt again by a man," or "I'm never going to get close and share my heart with another girlfriend, ever," or "I'm never going to be beautiful." Sometimes those things we say to ourselves as young children, even subconsciously, are the very things that shape our adult lives—we just don't realize it. So when we wonder, *Why can't I ever have a successful relationship?* our little child answers, *Because I said I never would.*

And so begins the frustrating self-destruction game. It's frustrating because even though we're playing it, we don't seem to know the rules for it. As we begin to peel back the layers of negative feelings about ourselves and as we remember and see that we are God's beloved creations, we gain the goodness of God's healing balm of love. He loves us. He created us. So what's not to like?

That's what keeps me running back to Him. I constantly want more of His gracious, love-enriched healing balm. When I'm able to see myself as He sees me, I also find and embrace that child I once was. She's held up under so many layers; she's been strong for so long. And now she's tired, and she's ready for some- one to lift off the weight of her mis- guided shame and mistaken blame and take care of her.

He loves us. He created us. So what's not to like?

These thoughts reinforce for me what Madeline L'Engle said about wholeness. As we heal and embrace *all* of who we are, she said, we begin to realize that we are six *and* forty-six. We are sixteen *and* we are thirty-one. We are adults with a history, and that history has helped make us who we are. If we hide behind layers of guilt, shame, or destructive habits, those layers can further alter our percep- tion of who we are.[1] As Titus 1:15 puts it, "To the pure, all things are pure, but to those who are corrupted and do not believe, nothing is pure. In fact, both their minds and con- sciences are corrupted."

When I felt like a pure and innocent little girl, I thought everyone else in the whole wide world was pure too. I was too young to understand, too young to believe any dif- ferently, so when I was corrupted by abuse, my mind and conscience were corrupted, too, like a corrupted computer file that no longer functions properly.

"IT WASN'T YOUR FAULT"

I felt at least one of my emotional layers fall away when I'd learned enough about abuse victims to look back at the blonde-haired, blue-eyed little girl I used to be and say, "It wasn't your fault. It wasn't because of what you looked like. It wasn't because of anything you did or didn't do, said or didn't say. It was because a bad person made evil choices and inflicted hurt upon you. For a long time, you blamed yourself and kept that hurt hidden because you didn't know any better. But underneath those layers of blame and shame, the hidden hurt grew. And eventually it infected all the other parts of your life. But none of it was your fault. You were a victim. But no more."

> *Underneath those layers of blame and shame, the hidden hurt grew. And eventually it infected all the other parts of your life. But none of it was your fault.*

Believe me; it feels good when those layers begin to fall away and healing starts. But just like the two-sided layers themselves, there's another side of letting those layers go. It's the fact that the healing doesn't happen suddenly and then it's done once and for all. Healing is a process, and it's hard work. Or maybe I should say it's challenging. Here's why.

Now that I've been through years of counseling, now that I feel restored to my rightful place as one of God's beloved creations, now that many of the layers have been peeled away . . .

now I have a responsibility to apply what I've learned. I've layered myself with knowledge and understanding I didn't have back then, when I was layering myself with food and misguided feelings. I can't claim ignorance anymore. Yet it's a struggle for me not to lament my body. I wish I was thinner, wish I would make healthier choices, wish I didn't love food so much. Yet so often I can't quite seem to muster the strength and courage to do the very thing I need to do.

I'm right there with the apostle Paul, who wrote, "I do not understand what I do. For what I want to do I do not do, but what I hate I do" (Romans 7:15). Or as translated in the SP (Sandi Patty) version: "Why the heck did I just eat that cookie when I didn't really want to, but I ate it anyway, knowing I didn't want to eat it?"

I backslide and make mistakes. When the stress piles up, when I'm tired and feeling sorry for myself, I'll reach for those cookies, darn it. I know I will.

But maybe, just maybe, next time, I'll think before I eat.

And maybe I'll *choose* to just eat one.

TWO SIDES OF HEALING HURTS

There are two ways to look at the two-word title of this chapter: as verb-plus-noun or as noun-plus-verb. In this book I'm sharing the hurt I've felt as I've moved beyond woundedness and begun the healing process. And although I certainly don't intend it as a how-to book, it may be that by reading my story you may get some ideas or encouragement about how you can begin healing your hurts as well.

It's been my experience that woundedness attracts woundedness; when you've been through something hurtful, you can often recognize it in others, and it's natural to either seek help—or offer it. That's the way I feel about the wounded women who share their hearts with me at the book table or signing booth after a concert or conference. Maybe we can see each other's hurting hearts in a way non-wounded people can't.

When we only have a few seconds to share our stories with each other, let's cut through the layers and speak right from the heart, okay?

When one of them tells me she's spiritually broken and emotionally stuck, she knows I understand, because I've been there. I want to wrap my arms around her and let her know I care. But I also hope that maybe my life experience can be an encouragement to her. I hope she'll see the happy life I'm living today and realize there's hope beyond her hurts as well.

I love it when women feel safe enough around me to share the challenges they're facing—or to tell me how my story has affected them or caused them to think.

To be honest, the comments I'd rather not hear are things like, "Oh, Sandi, you are beautiful! How could you think you're not?" Or "Sandi, you don't need to lose any weight. You're just fine as you are. God loves you as you are." Or

"Sandi, you've got to try this new diet product I (a) discovered, (b) developed, or (c) sell for only $49.99 a box."

After what I've been through, those kinds of comments sound shallow and insincere to my ears. I feel the layers going up and the authenticity fading, both for me and for the other person. When we only have a few seconds to share our stories with each other, let's cut through the layers and speak right from the heart, okay? Let's commiserate together because we both know that healing hurts. Or let's be sincere and honest with each other about the ways we've experienced healing hurts.

UNDERSTANDING LIFE
BENEATH THE LAYERS

I love to be around people who understand what it's like to live underneath the layers. One of those people was the therapist who followed me out the doors—and then back inside—on my first day at the mental hospital. After my dramatic exit and return, she helped me settle down and get to work. But I laid some ground rules right off the bat.

"I'm not going to sing while I'm here," I told her. "Don't ask me to. Don't expect me to. I'm not here to sing. I'm here to get my life back, so just don't even ask. It's my choice, and I am choosing *not* to sing." (Oh, I felt so assertive!)

"Okay," she said. "I've got it. No singing."

She moved right on to the first stage of our work together,

helping me identify some of the layers I'd been hiding behind. It was exhausting—emotionally, mentally, spiritually, physically. Every way it could be exhausting, it *was*. The first couple of days I wore my work clothes, some comfy old sweats, and I did nothing more than brush my teeth and splash water on my face before I showed up in her office each morning.

Then one day, probably the third day I was there, we went through some deep, dark stuff. Stuff that surprised me by the level of pain it inflicted. That evening I fell into bed, depleted but happy. I'd had what I considered a breakthrough. It was as though that little lightbulb came on in my head, and a little voice in my mind shouted, "Eureka! I'm healed!"

The next morning I bounced out of bed, pulled on clean sweats, dragged out my makeup bag, and put on what I call my "full face." We're talking concealer, eye shadow, blush, eye liner, mascara, the whole thing. I trotted down to the therapist's office, ready to thank her for her help, hear her pronounce me completely cured, and then head back home again to Indiana.

Instead she sat silently for a moment, taking in the glamorized Sandi. "Hmmm," she mused. "And what are we hiding today?"

Because she was the professional, and I was the patient— and a "newby" at mental-hospital residency—she was accus-

She sat silently for a moment, taking in the glamorized Sandi. "Hmmm," she mused. "And what are we hiding today?"

tomed to these *eureka!* moments early in the treatment. I thought we'd finally generated enough hurt to heal me. She knew we were only beginning. We got back to work. I never took out my makeup bag again while there.

On my last day, I sat with my group of fellow patients and the professionals who'd walked with us through the first steps of healing our hurts. We went around the circle, one by one, saying how much their help and friendships meant to us. But when it was my turn, I didn't speak. Instead, I gave them the only gift I had, and it was my choice, directly from my heart. I sang for them.

So what do I need now?

I need to keep singing, and meaning, the words of the song I sang that day: "Precious Lord, take my hand, lead me on . . ."

So what do you need now?

I need _____

_____

_____

6

Un-Layering Loved Ones

We do not know what we ought to pray for,
but the Spirit himself intercedes for us
with groans that words cannot express.

—ROMANS 8:26

The last few years have been tumultuous ones for our blended family. Together we've soared through the highest highs and grieved the hardest hurts. And in the process, I've seen my loved ones recognize and leave behind some layers—and pull on some new ones.

Things got off to an exciting start in May 2005 when we ecstatically celebrated the college graduation of my oldest daughter, Anna, and her fiancé, Collin, followed closely by three (count 'em, *three*) high school graduations as my twins Jennifer and Jonathan and Don's son, Donnie, received their diplomas.

Even before all the confetti had settled, we were once again swept up into a joy-filled whirlwind surrounding Anna and Collin's beautiful wedding—with parties, showers, and receptions—and all of us helping move them into their new place.

We had barely caught our breath after the wedding excitement when the three high school graduates headed off to college, and of course, they needed Mom and Dad's help to move all their stuff into their dorms. (And do freshmen ever get assigned to a *low* floor in the dorms? Noooooo. That would be way too easy.)

And then, as we enjoyed the joyful glow of those happily completed transitions—graduations, a wedding, college enrollment, and the start of school for the younger kids—there came a phone call that turned our world upside down.

It was Don's former wife, Michelle, calling from her home in Michigan. She'd been valiantly battling cancer for eight years. Each time the cancer came back, she'd successfully fought it off and carried on with a productive and happy life. But this time was different. This time the doctors told her the cancer was winning.

"They say I have six months," she told us.

NECESSARY LAYERS

Let me take a break here to do a quick who's who in our family. While I proudly lay claim to all eight children in my household, I only gave birth to four of them: Anna, twins Jennifer and Jonathan, and Erin. Michelle launched Donnie, Aly, and Mollie. Don and I adopted Sam in 1996.

For a while, all the kids lived with Don and me in Indiana. My kids spent lots of time with their dad, who lived across town, and Don's kids spent summers and holidays with Michelle in Michigan.

When Michelle was diagnosed with cancer eight years earlier, Mollie permanently moved to Michigan to live with her mother. After Michelle called in August 2006 to break the terrible news that the cancer had returned, Aly also moved to Michigan.

Donnie, who had just started college in Indiana, instantly made plans to move to Michigan too. But his mother asked him to reconsider. She told him the one thing she'd always wanted to do was to go to college. She urged him not to withdraw but to continue his studies. To honor her request, Donnie stayed in school.

Michelle died in January, five months after she broke the news to her children.

It's a hard, hard thing to see children—even almost-adult children—grieve. My heart ached for Donnie, Aly, and Mollie. They were understandably devastated by the news, and all of us hurt with them and for them. And yet, as we surrounded them with all the love and support we knew how to give, we also saw them handle their grief in a very mature, love-filled way. They knew they couldn't give in to their sorrow and simply

I watched them pull on protective layers, those necessary layers we all must don at times in our lives.

curl up in a corner and weep for the next year as they proba-bly felt like doing. Instead, I watched them pull on protective layers, those necessary layers we all must don at times in our lives. They are layers that keep the outside world from seeing the raw, tender wounds in our hearts.

After Michelle's call in August, those necessary layers let her kids manage their real feelings so they could work hard on school assignments and activities, spend time with their friends, and get through each day, sometimes one hour at a time, acting as though they were "normal" teenagers whose hearts weren't really breaking. It's how almost all of us react when we're dealt such a blow. It's normal.

The problem comes, though, if those layers stay in place too long or become too hardened or lead to unhealthy hab-its. I have no professional credentials that gave me insights into the layers I saw my stepchildren putting on after their mother's death. But I do have twenty-some years' experi-ence as the mother of many, combined with many years of personal therapy that helped me understand my own layers. Given that disclaimer—and with the kids' permission—I'd like to share some thoughts about the layers I saw them acquire. I hope that by sharing my family's experiences, you may gain insight into your own family members' layers so you'll know how best to help them.

After attending almost all of her school years in our hometown here in Indiana, Aly moved to Michigan during her senior year of high school to be with her mother during those last few months. That meant she was not only coping with seeing her mother succumb to a terminal illness but also enrolling in a new school, making new friends, jumping into new activities, and beginning what must have seemed like a whole new life. She had lots of friends and was heavily involved in her school in Indiana. She gave up a lot to move to Michigan. But she did it all with great spirit and enthusiasm. Never once did I detect even the tiniest bit of self-pity in her attitude.

Moving to Michigan was her choice; she wanted to be with her mother, and if being with her mother required some hard stuff, changing schools and all, then so be it. Even though I know it was hard on her emotionally in so many ways, she never, ever complained.

Now, of course, as a layering investigator, I know there are good and bad sides to that never-complain attitude. Aly is quick to sweetly say to anyone who expresses concern about her, "Oh, I'm fine. Really." Then she quickly changes the subject. She tends to pull on a smiling mask when I know there are tears right beneath the surface. I also see her layering herself with too many commitments—way more activities than one human being could ever keep up with. I'm guessing that the busyness keeps her from finding herself alone in a quiet place where the sadness of her mother's death can penetrate the layers and reopen her wounded heart. I suspect she believes if she can just stay busy enough, she can keep the sadness at bay.

She became so busy that she actually had to be hospitalized with mono for several days and, of course, had to slow the pace of her life. When we incur that kind of pain, says Marilyn Meberg, we tend to bury it alive, rather than dead-and-finished-with. Then it has a way of burping up on us at unexpected moments and in unexpected ways. That's what happened with Aly. Even though she tried to bury the pain with layers of busyness and overcommit-ment, it was just too great, and her body finally said "enough."

Those temporary layers pro-tected Aly during the freshest part of her grief. But I quickly saw her making strides to put the layers in their proper place. For instance, she readily admitted that overcommit-ment was a problem for her. Those relentless demands of all the busy-ness, which has tended to be a problem for her for a long time but intensified after her mother's death, meant she sometimes didn't finish what she started.

As a layering investigator, I know there are good and bad sides to that never-complain attitude.

But last year she showed impressive maturity by iden-tifying this layer and pushing it away. She had enrolled as a music major, and in a few weeks, as all the activities and requirements started piling up, she had second thoughts and considered changing. But then she told me, "You know what, Sandi? I've done that all my life—jumped into something and then changed my mind and not fol-lowed through. But not this time. I'm sticking with it."

Isn't that something? It's not the fact that she's

continuing as a music major although that makes me happy. Don and I don't care what she majors in; we just want her to find a career that makes her happy. The thing that pleases us both at this point is that she realized how she was layering herself in unhealthy ways, and she recognized how those layers were affecting her.

LAYERING TIGHTLY
SO NO TEARS GET THROUGH

Aly's older brother Donnie, now a sophomore in college, has surrounded himself with friends and laughter. He has always been the comedian in the family, and I've watched as he seems to have intensified that role in some ways since his mother's death. It's harder for guys to get through turbulent emotions because they don't want their tears to show, and they'll layer themselves tightly to make sure no tears get through to the surface. But those layers, even layers of laughter, can become toxic if they're left in place too long and smother out the real feelings hidden underneath.

Even layers of laughter can become toxic if they're left in place too long and smother out the real feelings hidden underneath.

Very often, if you look deep enough into a comedian's story, you see that he or she has also layered the pain with laughter.

It can become very therapeutic to work through that layer of laughter and understand how it's hiding your true feelings. Not that we want comedians to stop laughing—and making us laugh in the process. But identifying and understanding how layers are at work in our lives is always beneficial, even for those who seem to be harmlessly layered in laughter.

In contrast to Donnie and his typical male reluctance to let his feelings show, there's sweet Mollie, the youngest, who knows what Lana Bateman means when she says we should lean into our feelings. When the sadness hits Mollie, she weeps. She lets it out, whether she happens to be in the privacy of her room or the checkout line of the grocery store. Frankly, I think Mollie's handling her grief the most productively. She's letting it out, not holding it back. And she welcomes our understanding support and falls into our loving arms when the hurt gets too bad.

Having said that, I also see Mollie taking on the role of "the one who is always there" for her siblings. When I say she's the one who weeps, I don't mean to imply she's weak. The courage she has shown through the last few years, facing her mother's illness in such a down-to-earth, no-nonsense way, has inspired us all. She is one of the most selfless and caring people I know.

These three young loved ones of mine have survived an excruciating ordeal, one that will continue to affect them the rest of their lives. Unconsciously, they've pulled on some perfectly understandable layers of protection to get through these hard times: being active, being the life of the party, being there for others. These are all good things. And at this point I should add . . . so are chocolate chip cookies! It's just a matter of perspective and proportion. When these activities come as a temporary response to a hurtful situation, they can be protective and beneficiary. When they become permanently attached layers that keep others from seeing and knowing us as we really are, and when they keep us from a close, personal, authentic relationship with our Creator, that's when the protective layers become a prison.

When we focus so much on other people that we totally neglect ourselves, that's when the trouble starts. We want to feel purposeful, so we stay busy and we like to say yes to invitations to get involved in worthwhile activities. But when we do that to the point that we have no down time, we lose the opportunities we need to connect with ourselves and our God. When we work too hard giving others the gift of laughter, we lose sight of our need to authentically feel the pain that's eating away at our own hearts and let God's love and grace provide a balm for those wounds.

CLIMBING OUT OF THE COCOON

Seeing how the kids have layered themselves with good— but potentially imprisoning—things during this time of tough transition, I'm reminded of caterpillars. These little butter-flies-in-the-making are really vulnerable when they're fat little worms. They can't flutter out of the way of someone's foot or scurry away from a bird's hungry beak. But God didn't intend for them to be so vulnerable forever. So He taught them to build a cocoon of layers around themselves. Those layers are made of silk, which *can* be something good. Every woman I know loves the luxurious texture of silk against her skin.

But as the caterpillar layers itself with all this good silk, it creates something that eventually becomes distasteful. As far as I know, there aren't any creatures that like to eat cocoons. Some of them are hard and brittle; others have scratchy out-side coverings that also make them unappealing.

If the caterpillar remained inside those protective layers of good stuff, it would die. There comes a point when it has to peel back those layers and climb out of the cocoon. And when it does . . . oh, how wonderful! It becomes a butterfly.

Another illustration comes when we look at our brave military troops. When they're in a combat zone, both men and women layer themselves with body armor that helps protect them from the dangers around them. When they're at war, those layers are good. And they're not only good but downright essential—potentially lifesaving. But when those mommies and daddies come home to their families, they don't want *anything* layering them from the loving embraces of their loved ones.

WHEN PROTECTIVE LAYERS
BECOME A PRISON

As I've worked at peeling away my own layers, I've learned to look for the good in my loved ones' layers but also to help them prevent those "good" things from becoming a prison. And when I see behavior that seems unanticipated and unexpected in certain situations, I start wondering, *Hmmm. What's really going on here? Why would this person act this way* now?

I've gained quite a few insights about layering from Marilyn Meberg's new book *Love Me, Never Leave Me.* Marilyn identifies how abandonment issues can affect all of us, even those of us who never dreamed we'd ever felt abandoned. It can occur emotionally even when it doesn't occur physically, she said. And as a result, "strange feelings and behaviors sweep through me like a tidal wave clearing the beach." Those unexpected feelings and behaviors leave her "standing by myself on a lonely desert island of emotions wondering, w*here did* that *come from?*"[1]

That's exactly how I've felt as I've identified my own layers as well as those of my loved ones. For example, when Don and I were first married in 1995, everything was rosy. We enjoyed our lives together, and because we both have to travel with our jobs (he's the director of the Center for Character Development at Anderson University and also works in the community with the Character Counts program), we also enjoyed knowing we each had the freedom, understanding, and trust we needed to be apart.

Then something strange started happening. I noticed that as I would be leaving for a concert or meeting somewhere, Don's attitude toward me would subtly change. It was almost as though he was picking a fight with me. It was always over something trivial, things that ordinarily wouldn't have mattered. Maybe I'd forgotten to pick up his shirts at the laundry or left a mess of stuff on my side of the bathroom counter. Ordinarily it would be something that I would apologize for, and he'd answer, "It's okay. No problem."

But if it happened right before I was leaving to go to work out of town, I'd sense that he was more irritated than my easygoing Don normally would have been over my little acts of carelessness. And my sensing that in him left me standing there with Marilyn on that lonely island of emotions, wondering *where did* that *come from?*

Marilyn's book has given me fresh understanding of what I realized back then, when Don was layering himself. Back then, I finally understood—as Don and I talked about the situation and as he received his own professional counseling help. He had subconsciously responded to his wishing that I didn't have to leave with his layers of—as Patsy Clairmont puts it—"doesn't-bother-me-doesn't-bother-me-doesn't-bother-*me*." Rather than let himself feel the sad, unpleasant feelings of my leaving, he pulled on a layer that basically said, *Doesn't bother me. I'm* glad *you're leaving! In fact, I'm going to leave* you *(emotionally) before you can leave me.*

Rather than be vulnerable, it was easier for him to put up

a false front, pull on that layer. Looking back, his unexpected behavior reminds me of something I wrote in my journal as I was thinking about how my own old layers tended to push people away from me. I wrote, "I'm getting the ultimate protection, and yet that protection has become a prison. I'm creating the ultimate excuse for people to not like me."

If people don't like me, it means they don't know me, don't hang out with me. And *that* means they have no reason to leave me because they aren't there with me. Unless you've experienced and identified those layers creeping up around you, then you probably think this is really improbable and illogical thinking. And it is. But that doesn't keep it from happening to lots of folks, including Don and me.

His attitude of I'm-leaving-you-before-you-can-leave-me rubbed up against my own layer of being a perpetual pleaser, never wanting anyone to be mad at me because that meant something bad was going to happen. So we had these issues colliding with each other.

THE HURT OF GETTING LEFT

Slowly we learned—and Marilyn's book reinforces the lesson—that some of this comes from Don's adoption as an infant, as well as his adoptive dad dying when he was still a young boy. He was brought up in a warm and wonderful home as a beloved only child. But in her book Marilyn says, "Either consciously or subconsciously, all adopted

kids have to deal with the idea that they were given away."
The same thing can happen when a parent dies or divorce
separates a parent from the children or when a job or duty
requires parents to be away for an
extended time. What these kids subconsciously feel, Marilyn says, is
that they "got left."

*Most of us have
grown up learning
that we need to
hide our most
vulnerable feelings.*

Getting left hurts. But most of us
have grown up learning that we need
to hide our most vulnerable feelings.
So we pull on layers of emotional
and behavioral protection to hide
those feelings—and keep ourselves
from being hurt again. Now Don and I knew why his attitude
toward me changed as I left on a trip. And by knowing, we
could both recognize that layer when it reappeared.

And it *did* reappear, but in a way I hadn't anticipated
(although now I wonder why I didn't).

During the last few years, my work schedule has gotten
heavier. As a result, good-byes at our house have become
commonplace events that are almost as routine as they are for
someone who has a regular nine-to-five office job. Typically
there are hugs and kisses, then I unceremoniously head out
the door.

But something interesting happened not long ago, just a
few months after Michelle's death.

I started noticing that the day before I was scheduled
to leave, eleven-year-old Sam was very gently distancing

himself from me. Sam is the youngest of our blended bunch of eight children, the child we adopted after deciding we had room in our hearts for another child in addition to Don's three and my four. In our house it became a custom that Don or I—or both of us—would stop by each kid's room at bedtime and offer to chat. This year, with the six older children gone, these visits are more frequent since there are only two of them left—Erin and Sam—to share Mom and Dad's attention.

We really love sharing a few minutes together before these two fall asleep, talking or reading together, recapping the day, or just sharing a few thoughts before bedtime. We don't follow this practice every night, but many nights we do.

So as usual, one night before I was heading out the next morning, I stopped by Sam's doorway and asked, "Hey, buddy, you want me to cuddle with you a minute?"

He was lying on his bed, reading a book. "No, Mom, that's okay," he said. "I'm fine."

No big deal. I knew he was really into his book, and I didn't think anything about it. Part of the tradition is that you can opt out of the bedtime chitchat sessions anytime you want to without causing a fuss or hurting the other person's feelings.

But when the same thing happened the nights before my next couple of trips, I did think that was odd. "I'm good," Sam would say when I came by at bedtime and offered to snuggle. He wasn't being unkind, just sort of self-sufficient, you could say.

Usually when I leave for the airport, Sam is still asleep or already at school. But on one of those mornings after the self-sufficient "I'm-good" response to my offer to chat the night before, Sam happened to be home as I was leaving. We'd had our hugs and kisses, and I was stepping through the door to the garage when I felt Sam's arms close around me again.

"Mom, I don't want you to go!" he said.

"Mom, I don't want you to go!" he said. "Why do you have to leave me?"

I put down my bags and hugged him back. "Honey, is something wrong?" I asked.

"I just don't want you to go," Sam said, his face buried in my neck.

The first thing that came to mind was that same question Marilyn identified: *Where did* that *come from?*

ABANDONMENT ISSUES

It didn't take long for me to put two and two (or rather, father and son) together. Like Don, Sam was adopted. So he, too, probably had those abandonment issues Marilyn talked about. He had just watched three of his siblings struggle through the death of their biological mother. All of those thoughts swirled through his young mind, and actually seeing me physically walk out the door with my traveling clothes on and my luggage in tow triggered a different response in Sam than our usual good-night kiss the night before or a quick, lighthearted hug when he left for school before I left for the airport.

That day, all those issues ganged up on Sam and, I think, took us both by surprise. I stayed and talked to him awhile. He was upset, true. But I didn't hear that little note of true anguish that indicates genuine despair. You moms know what I mean. As the mother of eight children, I've developed what I believe is some extra-sensory perception over the years, and I cranked up my sensors to full alert that day as Sam asked me to stay. I didn't hear that "thing" in his voice that only parents can hear, that little something that says, *This is a big deal, Mom. Something's really wrong.*

That day, I pushed back Sam's layers and understood his heart. I assured him that I loved him with every breath of my being and that I wasn't abandoning him. I was just taking a little trip and would be back in less than forty-eight hours. Then I left and went to work. (But not without a few tears of my own, I might add.)

I didn't hear that little note of true anguish that indicates genuine despair.

Since then I've made sure that whenever I'm home and Sam wants or welcomes attention from Don or me, he gets it. And we've even talked to his school about ways we might do some partial homeschooling next year so that Sam could travel with me more frequently. Most of all, I've wanted to make him see that I hear and understand his authentic feelings, and I'm responding to them. We've talked about those abandonment issues that come from adoption, and he's learning to recognize the layers he pulls on in response to those issues when they arise.

I contrast this with another stage Sam is going through, one that many kids endure. As a popular sixth-grader, he's often invited to sleepovers at friends' homes, and he loves packing his bags and heading off for a fun time at his buddy's house. But it's not uncommon at all to be awakened by the phone ringing at, say, 1 a.m., and to hear that Sam has a stomachache and needs to come home.

When Anna was younger, I used to make a very big deal about her going to a friend's house for an overnight stay and then *staying* there. She used to have "stomach issues" just like Sam does now, and honestly, I wasn't nearly as understanding. I even told her one time that if she chose to stay then she could *not* call me in the middle of the night or she would get a spanking. And yes, that 1 a.m. phone call came, and we picked her up. And yes, I punished her. *UGH!!* That's so awful to write now. Let me just say, I've learned a lot about parenting since then, and it shows because my approach with Sam is so different.

Anna has even said she remembers that awful night being significant in her own defensive, destructive "layering" because that night she decided she wasn't going to upset people anymore by speaking her mind. She would just do whatever it took to make everyone happy, happy, happy.

Oh my, oh my, oh my! What was I thinking?! I'm so sorry for that misguided attempt to force my sweet daughter to "grow up and accept the consequences of her choices." That's a good plan, but my methods of "helping" her do that backfired, to say the least.

Fortunately, Anna now recognizes how that incident affected her. We've talked about it many times, and I have apologized for it again and again. It's a painful thing to remember, but I firmly believe that we need to *understand* the past in order to put it behind us. *Then* we can forget it. Now Anna and I have both learned a strong lesson, and we're moving forward with wisdom we didn't have in the past. We're following the apostle Paul's lead, "Forgetting what is behind and straining toward what is ahead . . . [pressing] on toward the goal to win the prize for which God has called me heavenward in Christ Jesus" (Philippians 3:13–14).

> ✣
>
> *I asked Sam, "If your stomach had a voice, what would it be saying?"*

Now, having mothered a houseful of other kids in between Anna and Sam, I know these late-night stomachache phone calls from a friend's house are not unusual. All parents get them, I'm sure. But again, we need to use our mothering radar and make sure there isn't something else going on, a problem that may arise from something other than just missing Mom and Dad.

So I asked Marilyn's advice about how to sift through the layers and discern whether this was a routine childhood stage or something bigger. She suggested that I ask Sam, "If your stomach had a voice, what would it be saying when you get sick at a friend's house?"

He replied without a moment's hesitation. "It would say, 'Sam! Lay off the burritos!'" he told me.

So what do I need now?

I need to be a little slower to assess my loved ones' unexpected responses—to take a moment to ask, where did that come from? I need to peel back the protective layers that may be causing their unanticipated and unpleasant responses to specific situations and embrace their vulnerable hearts with love.

So what do you need now?

I need _____

_____

_____

7

One Choice Away from Heading in the Right Direction

Whether you turn to the right or to the left, your ears will hear a voice behind you, saying, "This is the way; walk in it."

—ISAIAH 30:21

My dad, Ron Patty, was the youngest of nine kids. When he was a boy, he and his buddies would play football in the street of their small-town neighborhood. Invariably, someone would miss a catch or kick the ball too far, and then their one and only football would land in Old Lady Russell's yard.

This was not a good thing. Old Lady Russell had a "thing" about her yard, and she obviously didn't like kids either because if she caught one of the boys sneaking into her yard to get the ball back, she'd come out and rant and rave at them. The boys would move down the street to play for awhile, but eventually they'd end up back in front of her house, and inevitably the ball would land in her yard again.

The boys would draw straws or flip a coin or in some other
way decide who the unlucky fellow was who would have to
sneak into her yard to get the ball,
but Old Lady Russell apparently
had nothing better to do than stand
by her window and watch for the
trespasser to arrive. She'd fly out
the door, ranting and raving as the
poor kid grabbed the football and
hightailed it down the street.

He told his mom
what had happened.
She listened
attentively, nodding
and empathizing.

One day she decided she'd teach
those ornery boys a lesson. When
the ball landed on her lawn, she was ready for it. She trotted
out the door, snatched the ball up off the grass, and disappeared with it into her house.

No more football.

None of the boys was brave enough to go knock on Old
Lady Russell's door to ask for their football back. They knew
what the answer would be. The youngsters headed home,
dejected and miserable.

My grandmother, Grace Patty, noticed that Dad had
come home in the middle of the afternoon. She watched as
he collapsed into a heap in the chair and miserably slapped
his ball cap against his knee.

"What happened, Tyke?" she asked her young son, calling him by his family nickname.

He told his mom what had happened. She listened attentively, nodding and empathizing. "That's too bad, son,"

she said. "I know how you all enjoy playing with that football."

"Yeah, well that's over and done with now," Dad said morosely.

Grandma returned to the kitchen, and Dad slumped around the house. Pretty soon, though, he smelled something. His mom was baking a cherry pie. Well, that cheered him up some. He loved his mom's cherry pie.

But just as his appetite was at its peak and he spotted the pie cooling on the kitchen table, Grandma Grace (oh, how perfect her name was!) threw him for a loop. She sat the pie on a tea towel inside a cardboard box and handed it to Dad.

"Tyke, I thought I'd make a cherry pie for Old Lady Russell. Can you take it over to her house?"

"Mom! Are you crazy? There's no way I'm taking her a pie," Dad said. "She's a mean old lady, and she doesn't deserve a pie. Did you not hear me say she stole our football? And besides that, she'll probably kill me if I come into her yard, let alone if I knock on her door."

Grandma acted like she didn't even hear him. "I was just thinking she's probably lonely since she lives all by herself," she said. "I know it's hard to make yourself cook when there's just one person. I'll bet she would enjoy a cherry pie. So just tell her it's from you and that you were thinking about her. Don't ask for the football back. Just say you're sorry and you didn't mean to make her mad and would she like a pie."

So with great fear and trepidation, Tyke carried the

cherry pie down the street and through the gate into Old Lady Russell's yard. He balanced the box on one knee as he nervously knocked on the door. Then, when she came to the door, he stuck out the box and said, "This is a cherry pie from me and my mom. We thought you might like it."

Well, Old Lady Russell just melted.

She invited Dad in. And although he still wasn't sure she wasn't luring him in to kill him (and, for heaven's sakes, we wouldn't send our kids into a stranger's house today!), Dad went on in. They had a little visit, and she even offered to cut him a piece of the pie. Then she gave him the football back. And from that day forward, the kids never had a problem with Old Lady Russell. In fact, she would occasionally sit on her front porch and watch with great delight as the neighborhood boys played their football games.

FINDING A CHINK IN THE ARMOR

We don't know what caused Old Lady Russell to layer herself with a shell of hardened bitterness that kept her isolated from her neighbors and constantly mad at the children who played in her street. But we do know the magic tool that penetrated those layers. It was a woman named Grace who chose to extend *grace* to her unpleasant neighbor.

What a lesson Dad learned that day. It's one he never forgot. One that he taught to his children, including a daughter named Sandi (and one that I've taught my children too). It was a lesson that illustrated the power of a random act of kindness—a random act of grace.

I love that story. It reminds me that no matter how hardened others' protective layers of emotions and behaviors may be, no matter how unpleasant they may seem, there's always a chink in the armor.

Do you know where we got the term *Achilles' heel*? According to Greek mythology, Thetis dipped her infant son Achilles in some kind of protective coating—some say the River Styx, some say a vat of liquid gold—and that layer, whatever it was, completely protected him from all wounds and injuries. Completely protected him, that is, except for the place where his mother grasped his heel as she held him upside down and dipped him. There, on his heel, there was no protective layer. And although he became the greatest of mythical warriors, it was there, on his heel, where a fatal blow landed, ending his life.

There's always a weakness in our layers, a spot where we're vulnerable to something that slips in and makes a difference. For so many of us, that one spot is vulnerable to *kindness*.

There's always a weakness in our layers, a spot where we're vulnerable to something that slips in and makes a difference.

But kindness is not always the natural, instinctive way most of us respond to the hard, embittered, thoughtless, unappealing, or downright rude layers others present to us. No, a more common reaction to a bitter old lady who takes and keeps our kids' only football is to call her up and give her a piece of our mind. Or when her morning newspaper accidentally lands in our driveway instead of hers, to shred it and toss it over her fence. Or at least to glare at her as we drive past her house.

Uh-huh. That's the "natural" way we might want to respond to others' unattractive, hurtful layers. Let's face it: for one split second, it might feel mighty good to unload some angry words or deeds on someone who has just treated us or our kids unjustly.

Ah, but then what do we have to do when our conscience kicks in and our faith nudges our spirits? We turn to our gracious heavenly Father and repeat Jesus' amazing words: "Forgive us our debts, *as we also have forgiven our debtors*" (Matthew 6:12, emphasis mine).

Gulp.

It's all about *choice* and how we *choose* to respond.

Choice is such a big issue for many victims of abuse. At the mercy of our abusers, we felt we had no choice but to submit to what they did to us. As a result, as adults, many of us tend to get nervous, or even panicky, whenever we perceive that our choice is being taken away from us. We feel trapped. Stuck. If we *think* we don't have a choice, we find ourselves incapable of making a choice when, in fact, choices *are* offered to us. It's all a matter of perspective.

AN INVITATION TO DINNER

Given that mind-set, let me invite you to family dinner at our house. Just come as you are—or rather, as you *were*. We're going back a few years when all eight kids were at home almost every night. Just sit anywhere; we're very informal. We'll make room for you at our huge circular table in the breakfast nook that seats . . . well, it seats however many we need to squeeze in at one time. Usually ten, but it's been known to accommodate a virtual army of pizza-packing kids.

Tonight Nana and Papa Patty are joining us, and we're starting a new routine that Don and I are calling "high-low." As we eat, we're going around the table, asking each person to share his or her highest high and lowest low of the day. When the kids were little, this might mean that someone bragged about getting an A on the math test and then lamented that Suzy had sat by someone else at lunchtime.

It was simply a system we devised that nurtured family conversation and helped us connect with all eight kids. We cheered at their good news and cooed, clucked, and commiserated sympathetically as they shared the low points of their day.

I was surprised a day or two later when I was going somewhere with Mom and she said, "You know, Sandi, Daddy and I were talking about that new conversation-starter you're doing at dinner. It's really a good practice to have the kids remember and share the best thing that happened to them every day. What a good idea."

I could tell there was something else coming.

"But, honey, is it a good idea to also focus on the *hardest* thing that happened to them every day?" Mom continued. "Wouldn't it be better to forget the hard times and just focus instead on the good things that happen? You know, the blessings big and little that come to us every day? Isn't it better to keep on the sunny side, as the old song says?"

Mom's question took me by surprise—and made me think. Once again I looked for layers that might explain why she was encouraging me to keep my family's focus on the sunny side of life without acknowledging the darker things that happened to us.

My thought process took me back to my own childhood, and I realized that my brothers and I had grown up doing just what Mom was suggesting we do today: we had focused on all the good things in our lives—and there were many. We were surrounded by love and support and provided with a comfortable home, nice neighborhoods, and happy surroundings.

But the more I thought about it, the more I realized I had also grown up without knowing that I had a choice about expressing the

I realized I had also grown up without knowing that I had a choice about expressing the highs and lows in my own life.

highs and lows in my own life. At our house, we focused on the good. We were reared to be like the little kid in the story who was confronted with a pile of horse manure and happily started digging away, exclaiming, "I know there's gotta be a pony in here somewhere!"

It's a gift to be able to enjoy the rose and overlook the thorns, to watch for the rainbow even while the thunder is still booming and the lightning's still flashing. I appreciate that gift that was instilled in me by my parents.

Maybe it came from their own childhood layers when they grew up during the Great Depression and their families struggled through difficult economic situations that were harder than anything I ever experienced. Maybe it was because they spent so much of their lives in the spotlight, either as pastor and pianist of whatever church Dad was leading or as musical performers on stage. I do remember that when we started traveling and performing together as the Ron Patty Family, we kids were told over and over and *over* again to "Smile!" whenever we found ourselves in front of an audience.

Yes, that practice is a good one. It's also a silk cocoon, something protective that has the potential to become a prison.

I felt that I needed to "keep on the sunny side," hide the hard things, and layer on a happy smile.

I see now that as good as it was, that practice also kept me from seeing that I had a choice. I could have chosen to tell Mom and Dad about the low spots in my day. They would have listened to me and validated whatever I needed to tell them. But as I look back, I see that most of the time I didn't recognize that I had that choice. Instead, I felt that I needed to "keep on the sunny side," hide the hard things, and layer on a happy smile, no matter what I was feeling inside.

This is the way parenting is, isn't it? You think you're doing the absolute best thing for your kids, and then later, they go through counseling and find out that everything their parents sacrificed for them and did for them was wrong!

All joking aside, no one had a better upbringing than I did. I was blessed with the world's most wonderful parents, and they are living treasures to me today. They live a couple of blocks away from me and are lovingly involved in my life—and my family's well-being. Quite simply, we all adore them.

And because they've seen through all my layers and know the real me, they know they can speak freely and share their thoughts and wisdom even when it means gently questioning one of Don's and my parenting practices, such as the dinner-table high-low discussions. Likewise, I feel safe and secure in their love, so I was comfortable saying to Mom that day, "You know what, Mom? This really works for us. We want to know *everything* that's going on in the kids' lives, so we want to hear the good *and* the bad. We want to acknowledge with the kids that, yes, there are some days that aren't going to be very good. That's okay. It happens. Asking them to talk about it helps them feel free to not feel guilty if they have a bad day. Does that make sense?"

She nodded understandingly. And ever since then, she and Dad have been active participants in the round-table topics whenever they eat with us. (However, they almost always have an amazingly hard time remembering a low point to share.)

CREATING OPPORTUNITIES FOR CHOICES

When counseling helped me understand how important the matter of choice is to me, I made sure I wove lots of opportunities for my kids to make choices in their everyday lives.

Recently a phone call from Jonathan reminded me of that conversation with Mom several years ago about the high-low discussion. Jonathan was calling from his dorm room on the college campus across town. I said, "Hey, buddy, how's your day going?"

He said, "Well, it hasn't been anything spectacular." And immediately he started looking for something wrong as though there had to be some concrete reason why the day wasn't anything to brag about.

I said, "Jon, you know what? Sometimes days are just . . . daily days. There's nothing really wrong with them, and there's nothing spectacular with them, and that's okay."

He said, "Yeah, you're right. This was just a daily day."

I wanted him to know it was all right for him to admit his day had been kind of boring. It was important to me for him to know he had that choice. If he wanted to build it so it sounded like a fantastically wonderful day, that was okay. But he could also tell me it was a so-so day. I wasn't going to correct him and urge him to keep on the sunny side if the day wasn't all that bright.

I've done my best to make sure my kids feel they have choices. When they were little, those choices were minor and mundane: "Do you want to wear your red shoes today or your black shoes?" I wanted to nurture in them the understanding that they had a choice, and sometimes either choice is fine. Some days are red shoes days, and some days are black shoes days, and you know what? Either one is okay.

A friend follows this same practice but with even fewer guidelines. She said she and her little girl discuss what she's wearing to preschool the next day, and basically Sophie wears whatever she wants to wear as long as it covers all the things it needs to cover and isn't a safety issue or a distraction for her classmates and teachers.

"So what did she wear today?" I asked.

"Let's see," my friend said. "Today, I dropped her off wearing her leotard and tutu, a snow parka, and rain boots."

When our kids got older, Don and I never really said, "Here's your curfew. This is it, set in stone." Instead, anytime the kids were going out with friends or on a date, we would ask, "What time are you going to be home?" We put the responsibility on *them* to set a reasonable time and then stick with it. So on a school night they might say they were going to a friend's house to study and would be home by 9:30. On a special weekend night, they might say, "Well, we're gonna do this, then we're going there, so how about 12:15? Is that okay?"

> ❧
>
> *When a choice they made turned out well, they felt validated.*

If we weren't comfortable with what they planned, we'd have some discussion about it, but usually we agreed to what they set. I believe that empowered them, setting their own reasonable curfew. That's what choice does; it empowers people.

Then, when a choice they made turned out well—when they said they would be home at 12:15 a.m. and they *were* home by 12:15 a.m.—they felt validated that they were smart enough to handle some decision-making.

WHEN I THOUGHT
I DIDN'T HAVE A CHOICE

I believe that letting our kids choose their own curfews empowered them to make good decisions. In the same way, I have a sense of empowerment in this second part of my career that I didn't feel in my early days because I now understand that I, too, have choices. They're actually the same choices I had back then; the difference is that back then I didn't know I had them. I can name a dozen examples, but here are some that I've felt most dramatically.

The most obvious is that now I feel I'm *choosing* to sing. I know that probably sounds strange, but it's true. Only in the last ten years or so have I actively *chosen* to sing. I guess I've always known I *needed* to sing. Or I've been *expected* to sing or even *gifted* to sing. Therefore, I've sensed that I've *had* to sing.

Early in my professional career, I began feeling *obligated* to sing, even *forced* to sing by circumstances beyond my control. There were big bills to pay with several staff and band members depending on me and lots of equipment involved in my concerts. Sometimes my life felt like one giant snowball rolling down the mountain constantly gaining momentum, and I was powerless to stop it.

Here's an example of how out of control things were. When Anna was a tiny baby, less than a year old, she was given some medicine for an ear infection that she turned out to be highly allergic to. She was *really* sick, had a terrible fever, and ended up being hospitalized for several days. Things were really tense, and although she was expected to survive, during the first days of her reaction, there was no reassurance about that prognosis.

Her illness came while I was in the middle of a big, widely publicized national concert tour involving nightly appearances in different cities around the country. And I am ashamed now to say that I would leave my little baby every afternoon, climb onto a chartered jet, fly somewhere to do the concert, then fly back that night. As you can imagine, I was killing myself with constant exhaustion. But I kept on going.

I remember performing one concert and briefly attending a reception held afterward before rushing to the airport to fly home. I was very distracted and didn't feel I had performed well. I didn't want to be there, and I guess it probably showed.

At that reception, a woman came up to me and said, "You know, your concert was great, Sandi. But, honey, you need to be home with your little daughter."

I looked at her and said in all seriousness, "I didn't know I had a choice."

Can you believe that? I honestly didn't know I could choose to say, "You know what? I've gotta cancel these next three or four dates until I know what's going to happen because my little girl is sick, and I need to be with her."

I can hardly even think of that time now without feeling tears building up in my eyes. I wanted to be with Anna with all my heart, but I thought my obligation to my ministry should supersede a family emergency. I thought if I canceled concert dates, lots of people would be mad at me and that my career would be irreparably damaged. *I thought I didn't have a choice.*

CHOOSING TO SING

During those early days I also dreaded doing the "signing line," signing autographs and greeting fans after a concert, but I did it because I was "supposed to." I didn't realize I had a choice about doing autographs. It's all a matter of perspective. When I thought I didn't have a choice about signing autographs, when I thought that, above all, I had to keep from disappointing the public, I honestly resented my obligation to do it. I felt like people were taking from me, pulling off parts of me to keep for themselves.

This might sound strange, but one of the things I vowed to do in this book was to share my journey—mud, muck, and all. In that spirit, I must admit that my attitude about the signing line was one of the darker parts of the trip.

> The biggest changes have come about because I realize I can choose.

That has all changed now, and the biggest changes have come about because I realize I can *choose*. So now I look forward to the signing line. As exhausting as it is, physically and emotionally, I love the fact that I'm *choosing* to connect with these dear people, mostly women, who share their hearts with me as I've shared mine with them.

Similarly, I choose to sing now, and I love doing it. I eagerly anticipate every concert and every Women of Faith conference. But if an emergency arises at home or if I'm sick and my voice sounds like fingernails on a chalk board, I call and cancel. I know it inconveniences and disappoints a lot of people, and I still feel the effects of being a perpetual pleaser. So I do it only rarely. But when I'm up against a hard situation, I realize now that I can choose to apologize for the trouble and the hassle and then reschedule the event. Even though I don't like doing it, I'm happier knowing I have my priorities straight and I'm choosing to do what I need to do at that time.

There are times in our lives when we are given a glimpse of our emotional growth. So often *while* we are growing and getting past the difficult habits and issues, it's hard to see our progress right then, in the moment. It's like when my children were babies and I would take them for their regular doctor visits. I would always marvel at how much they had grown since the last time we had been there. I'd been with them every day, and I just hadn't noticed each incremental inch and ounce.

But eventually I started *seeing* their growth right there in that same doctor's office setting, maybe because I was watching for different things, seeing the same situation differently. For instance, when the kids were babies, I had to stand by the exam table so they wouldn't fall off. But as they got older, that became unnecessary. In fact, they quickly got to the point where they could climb up on the table themselves. I love going to the doctor with them now for check-ups (when they want me to) and reminiscing about their growth and what great kids they are.

This reminds me of a funny growth story about a friend of mine. Her son went to the same pediatrician all his life—even in high school and into his college years.

"Micah just really liked that doctor," his mom said. "Everyone knew him in that office, and the doctor knew him on sight. It was just a friendly, comfortable environment, and since Micah never had any serious health issues, there wasn't ever a need for some other kind of specialist. So he just kept going to the pediatrician."

Micah started worrying that the day would come when the doctor would tell him he needed to move on to a "grown-ups'" physician. But the doctor assured him as long as there were no special problems and as long as he could stand all the teasing as he sat in the doctor's lobby, waiting his turn with all the moms and tots, he could keep coming for simple checkups and illnesses such as colds. But Micah loved the teasing even when one of the nurses told him as she took his vital signs, "You know, Micah, I'm just not used to listening to a patient's heart with all this chest hair to deal with!"

OH! I DID IT!

My point (perhaps you were wondering how on earth we got on the issue of chest hair in a discussion of emotional and spiritual growth) is that our growth psychologically may not be as apparent as our physical maturity. But then something happens and we think, *Oh! I did it!* Just recently I had an opportunity to be in one of those circumstances, and I was amazed at how differently I responded than I would have done in the past.

The women in my signing line at Women of Faith conferences are, for the most part, warm, loving, and often funny, and they make wonderfully affirming comments and tell me insightful stories about their own imperfect pasts.

But every once in a while, there will be someone who just has to get something off her mind, and what she has to say is not warm, not loving, not funny, and certainly not affirming. Not too long ago, I was finishing up with my signing line during a conference break, and I noticed a young lady, perhaps in her mid-thirties, waiting quietly a little ways away. As I began to walk back to the elevator to return to the program, she asked if she could speak to me for a minute. I asked if we could walk and talk, and she said sure.

She said, "Sandi, you have a beautiful voice, but don't you think that just once you should sing to God and not try to entertain the people so much?"

Well, her question caught me completely by surprise. But because I've grown in the way I respond to such things, I took a quick moment to remember I had a choice in how I would answer her. And that was important to me.

You see, in times past, I probably would have apologized profusely to the woman and spent the next weeks— yes, *weeks*—with my mind in constant turmoil as I rehashed and reanalyzed the woman's comment. I would have anguished over my "failure" to be the Sandi Patty she wanted me to be. I would have worried how I might somehow do something differently so that I would never, ever disappoint *anyone* ever again.

I spoke up for the real Sandi, the one who used to hide out under the layers.

But I'm smarter now. I've grown, both emotionally and spiritually, as I've identified my layers and peeled away some of the most troublesome ones (while I continue to work on the rest!). Instead, I spoke up for the *real* Sandi, the one who used to hide out under the layers. I linked my arm through hers and pulled her close to me so I didn't have to speak very loudly. Then I said, "Oh, sweetie, everything I do is for God. When I'm on that stage, the things I share, the things I sing, are out of my own relationship with my heavenly Father. By sharing that relationship publicly, I hope I'm encouraging those who are listening. I can't ignore the audience, true. But what I'm doing is inviting them to come along and worship with me."

I could have kept my mouth shut, and maybe some would say I should have done so. But I considered it an opportunity for what felt to me like a teaching moment. More importantly, I had a choice to tell the woman how I honestly felt. And when I did that, as graciously as I knew how, let me just say, it felt *good* because I was sharing my true and honest feelings. I was sharing my authentic self.

The incident also reminded me of something I heard my pal Chonda Pierce say. Ironically, someone told her just the opposite of what the woman had told me. She said something like, "Chonda, when you're on stage, you seem to be working heart and soul for the Lord."

Well, that lady was wrong about Chonda just as "my" woman was wrong about me. And instead of saying a simple, "Thank you, that's so sweet," Chonda eagerly chose to set the woman straight: "Oh, no, honey, I *live my life* for the Lord," she said. "I *work* for those people out there in the audience."

If you're the kind of person who's always been able to express your heart, these statements probably don't seem like that big a deal. But to someone like me who's been a perpetual pleaser, who for most of my life couldn't stand the thought of disappointing anyone, it *is* significant.

Now when I have something on my heart that needs to be expressed, or whenever I'm in a situation where my actions or decisions have been misinterpreted, I don't want to cover up my real self with layers of excuses or insincere apologies or dismissive comments.

As much as I can, I want to share my honest self with those around me. I want to have the kind of honesty that comes out as an expression of genuine love for my fellow human beings. Not ooey-gooey, syrupy gushing or automatic apologizing, as I might have done in the past if, for instance, someone misinterpreted my on-stage performance and suggested I try performing for God instead of my audiences. What I choose to do now, whenever I can, is share the kind of authentic communication Francis Schaeffer wrote about in his book *The God Who Is There*. He wrote, "Genuine love, in the last analysis, means a willingness to be entirely exposed to the person to whom we are talking."[1]

THE JOY OF CHOICE—
AND THE CHOICE OF JOY

It's all about perception. Sometimes hard things happen to us when we sense that we don't have a choice. Remember in the last chapter when I was describing how Sam ran after me as I headed out the door for a trip? If my mothering radar had detected that certain, from-the-heart, Mom-I-need-you message in his voice that day, I would have picked up the phone and canceled the trip. Today, I *know* I have a choice. Even when it's one that's hard to make, I *do* have a choice.

That day, I sensed that Sam's clinginess wasn't serious, and I was right. Whenever I called home during that trip, either he or Don assured

> ❦
>
> *Even when it's one that's hard to make, I do have a choice.*

me everything was fine. When you learn that you *have* choices and learn *how to make them,* you eventually also learn to trust your instincts when you have to make hard decisions.

During the months when Michelle was very, very ill and Don was in Michigan with his kids, I canceled several dates so that I could be at home with Sam and Erin and also be near the older kids attending college across town. Those were dark, sorrowful days for our family, and although we have a dear friend who's been our kids' nanny throughout their entire lives, I knew that at that difficult time they needed Mom, not their nanny, as fond of her as they were.

You know, when you start recognizing the choices that are out there, it can make you a little, well, mischievous. Maybe, if you're a perpetual pleaser, as I spent much of my life being, you're also one who follows all the rules and never wants to do anything that might cause trouble—trouble being, in some cases, a raised eyebrow or an impatient sigh. I guess I was feeling a little of that I've-got-choices mischief all those years ago when we adopted Sam and I filled out the paperwork for the adoption agency. Sam's birth parents were a blend of African American, American Indian, and Caucasian heritages. So on that adoption form, when I got to the blank that said, "Race _____ ," I paused only a split second before I chose to write the answer that came straight from my heart if not from my head. I wrote, "HUMAN."

DECIDING OUR DIRECTION, ONE CHOICE AT A TIME

We began this chapter with a story about how my Grandma Grace found the chink in Old Lady Russell's hardened layers of emotional armor. I want to end it by reminding you of all the choices you have in your life. Grandma Grace and Old Lady Russell showed us both extremes: kindness and bitterness. We can choose how we respond to the situations that confront us throughout our lives. We don't *have* to respond the way we've always responded. We don't have to respond as others expect us to. We're just one choice away from heading in the right direction . . . or the wrong one. We *will* be held accountable, one way or another, for the choices we make.

We don't have to respond the way we've always responded.

I'm thinking of the day I picked Sam up from school and he

was angry and upset about something that had happened to one of his friends. "Mom," he said, "I just want to *hit* something."

I couldn't help but chuckle at his frustration. I thought how many times, when I'm upset about something, I think, *I just want to* eat *something!*

In our frustration, Sam and I are in the same boat. We're one choice away from heading in the right direction. If we give in to the urge to hit something or eat something, there will inevitably be negative consequences. But if we can make the right choice, well, then nobody gets hurt.

I took him to the batting cage that day because he *did* need to hit something—but something safe—and fun. Now that I think about it, I'll bet that batting cage business has witnessed a lot of anger over the years as people young and old have chosen to release their frustrations there in a productive way instead of causing injury to others, both physically and emotionally.

We're all one choice away from heading in the right direction. One choice away from falling from the course that is good and true. One choice away from hardening our layers of harshness, anger, disappointment, sorrow, false happiness, withdrawal, food, addiction . . . the list is endless. We're also one choice away from removing those layers bit by bit and easing their tight hold on us.

We decide our direction, one choice at a time.

Think about it: at any point in your life's journey, you're one choice away from heading in the right direction. Throughout our day we're offered choices—look for them; they *are* there. And every time we choose, we can decide to head the right direction, peeling back one of those layers a little bit more to reveal our real selves. Or we can decide to recede into the layers and shield ourselves away from authentic relationships with our loved ones and, most importantly, with God.

I know some people who wear a rubber band on their wrist and snap it gently whenever they're tempted to slide back into an addiction, whether it's "just one" cigarette or pill or drink or chocolate chip cookie. The pop they feel against their skin is simply a reminder that they're one choice away from heading in the right direction.

Most of us (now) know we have a choice, and most of the time, we know what the right choice is. The question is, are we strong enough to choose it?

REFUSE, REPLACE, REPEAT

Patsy Clairmont had to make some tough choices to overcome a longtime struggle with agoraphobia. She used a three-word principle to help her choose, one decision at a time, the right path. Those three words were *refuse, replace, repeat.*

She refused the negative thought that tempted her to make the wrong choice. She replaced the negative pull with something God assured her was true. And then she repeated that practice every time she was confronted by that mental fork in the road. Thinking about Patsy's advice, I chose to put it in practice this way. Looking in the mirror, I might think, *Oh, you are so ugly. Nobody could love you.* (I've already told you

I like myself from the inside looking out, but I'm still working on the outside looking in part.) But then I would *refuse*
that negative choice and choose instead to *replace* it with what
God (and Don) have convinced me is true: *Don is crazy about
me, and God loves me more than anything I could ever imagine.*
Then I *repeat* that truth again and again until I *know* without a
doubt that I'm headed in the right direction.

In what ways are *you* one choice away from heading in
the right direction at this very minute?

So what do I need now?

I need to always perceive that I'm one choice away from
heading in the right direction—and snap myself into
making the choice God would have me make even when
it's the hard choice. I know "I can do all things through
Christ who strengthens me" (Philippians 4:13 NKJV).

So what do you need now?

I need _____

_____

_____

8

Hard Layers

For we do not have a high priest who is unable to sympathize
with our weaknesses, but we have one who has been tempted
in every way, just as we are—yet was without sin.

—HEBREWS 4:15

As the mother of eight kids, I've read a *lot* of children's books, let me tell you! And many times, I get as much, if not more, out of the really excellent books as my kids do.

Among my favorites (and, coincidentally, also among the favorites of millions of other parents and children around the world) is the Chronicles of Narnia series by C. S. Lewis. He had a wonderful way of telling exciting, engrossing stories full of imaginative adventure while also sharing the most amazing insights and leaving behind indelible lessons.

My favorite book in Lewis's Narnia series is *The Voyage of the Dawn Treader.* As I think about the ways we layer ourselves with so many destructive and unhealthy things—food, alcohol, drugs, relationships, poor choices, overcommitment—I'm reminded of the experience one of the Narnia characters, a boy named Eustace, had in a dragon's lair. (And yes, it did occur to me that in Eustace's story, a *layer* and a *lair* were both things that caused problems for him.)

Eustace and I have several things in common. One is that we both tend to be self-centered hoarders. I've already admitted that I tend to hoard just-in-case food, like those snack bars I find myself shoving in my purse as I head out the door. But more importantly, I hoard *myself*.

I hoard my time, my sleep, my thoughts. Maybe that's yet another thing I've shared throughout my story that sounds strange, and you want to say, *Sandi, how can you hoard* time? *Time is the same for everyone. You can't stuff it away somewhere to use later.*

I hoard my time, my sleep, my thoughts.

What I mean is, I shut myself away behind that time-hoarding layer and think, *I got up so early this morning for my flight. If I don't take a nap in my hotel room, I may get tired at tonight's concert.*

Well, yes, I may get tired. And yes, I need to be rested to give my best performance. But many times in that situation the truth is closer to this: It wasn't all *that* early when I got up. I've performed on a lot less sleep than what I've had in the last twenty-four hours. And maybe it would be a better use of time at that particular moment to reconnect with friends I haven't seen for a while who live in the area or are staying at the same hotel.

Honestly, it's sometimes a very hard thing for me to shake myself out of that kind of lay-up-in-my-lair thinking and instead call a friend to have lunch or a cup of coffee. I want that little bit of free time all for myself. But sometimes what I'm really doing is hiding behind a layer of selfishness, or even laziness. To go have lunch with my friend, I probably need to fix my hair or put on some makeup or change clothes . . . and it's so much easier to just lie around the hotel room in my comfy clothes.

So I consciously work at Patsy's plan of refusing, replacing, and repeating that attitude for a better one. I tell myself, *My heavenly Father knows all my needs. And just as He cares for the lilies of the field, He cares for me. If I really need rest or sleep or food or whatever, He'll make sure I get it. But that's not what's happening now. Right now I'm just hoarding myself and being lazy. And that's not a layer I want to hide behind.*

I refute that self-centered thought and replace it with one that says, "I'm so lucky that my dear friend is right here in the same hotel and we can spend some time together right now. Thank You, God!"

Eustace's layer of self-hoarding showed up in many ways. When the *Dawn Treader* was hit by a violent storm at sea and supplies ran low, Eustace manufactured some greedy self-talk that convinced him that the crew's decision to ration their water supply applied only to his fellow passengers, not to him. And when they finally managed to find safe anchorage, he slipped off to indulge himself in some pleasant self-time while the other passengers struggled to repair the ship, restock supplies, and perform dozens of other arduous tasks. He wandered off to explore and ended up falling asleep in a dragon's treasure-filled cave.

WAKING UP IN THE DRAGON'S LAIR

There, "sleeping on a dragon's hoard with greedy, drag-onish thoughts in his heart," Lewis wrote, Eustace himself became a dragon.

And how did Eustace *know* he'd become a dragon? He was layered in dragon skin, of course! And, almost like a badge of his selfish greediness, on his front leg (which the night before had been his arm) was embedded a gold bracelet he had claimed for himself after stealing it out of the treasure he'd found in the dragon's lair. The bracelet had been too big for his arm, but when he awoke as a dragon, it was much too small and cut very painfully into his front leg.

Horrified, he stumbled around on all fours, dragonlike, until one night he met a lion. Eustace didn't know it at the time, but this wasn't just any lion, either, but the great Aslan. If you don't already know, see if you can figure out who Aslan represents as I tell you the rest of the story.

The lion led Eustace to a well of clear, cold water on top of a mountain. Eustace longed to get into the water because he sensed it would ease the pain that was consum-ing him from the too-tight stolen bracelet. But the lion said he had to get undressed first.

Undressed? Eustace thought. *I'm a dragon. I'm not wearing any clothes.* Then he remembered that dragons, like snakes, shed layers of skin. So he started scratching at himself until he was able to peel away the ugly dragon skin.

But what do you know? Underneath that layer was another one . . . and another one. No matter how much Eustace tried, he couldn't seem to shed *all* the layers of rough, ugly dragon skin that would keep him from enjoying the cool, refreshing waters of the well.

> *What do you know? Underneath that layer was another one . . . and another one.*

That's when Aslan finally told Eustace he would have to let him, the lion, undress him. Eustace looked at the lion's long, terrible claws, terrified of how that might happen. But he was so desperate to get rid of his hard, knobby, ugly dragon skin that he quickly lay prostrate and vulnerable, finally willing to let the lion tear off the layers.

As the first claw tore into him, Eustace said, he felt as though he'd been stabbed in the heart. As Aslan peeled the old skin away, Eustace felt excruciating pain unlike any he'd ever experienced before. Yet even as the pain threatened to consume him, a wonderful sense of tender cleansing took hold. Eustace said it was like the feeling of picking at a scab: "It hurts like billy—oh but it *is* such fun to see it coming away."

When the old layers of ugly, hard skin were lying in piles beside Eustace, Aslan picked up the boy and threw

him into the waters of the well. And suddenly all the pain
was gone, and Eustace was a boy again.[1]

A JOY THAT'S WORTH THE PAIN

Oh, my! Just sharing the story again makes me tense with
anxiety as I feel, with Eustace, the stab of that mighty claw
piercing the ugly layers that hide my heart and ripping
them away. Then I sense the cold, rejuvenating Living
Water washing over me, and I feel myself being restored
to the original *me* God created.

With those baptismal waters still dripping from my tender, vulnerable, unlayered self, I lean into the love of my
Creator and begin again, sharing the true feelings of my
unadorned, unlayered heart . . . the
heart He put in me to hold His love
and share His grace.

I wanted to start this "Hard
Layers" chapter with Lewis's story
of how God peeled back the layers
of a dragon to restore a young boy
because it reiterates my belief that
only with God's help can we peel

*Only with God's
help can we peel back
all the layers that
burden our lives.*

back *all* the layers that burden our lives. We can try to do
it alone, picking and scratching at our knobby dragon skin,
but to really get rid of it, we have to present ourselves to
Him and allow Him to do His work in us.

And second, I share this story because it so vividly describes the great pain that sometimes comes as God peels back our layers and throws us into the well of Living Water. Aslan's claws ripping away Eustace's dragon skin represent the double-edged sword of truth described in Hebrews 4:12. While it cuts and hurts, it also heals.

Two thousand years after the writer to the Hebrews called this tool a sword, Eugene Petersen, paraphrasing the Bible into his popular *The Message* version, puts Hebrews 4:12 this way: "His powerful Word is sharp as a surgeon's scalpel, cutting through everything, whether doubt or defense, laying us open to listen and obey."

Yes, the anguish can be great . . . ahhh, but what comes next makes all that happens worth the pain. For what comes next is the extraordinary gift of new joy, new peace, and new life as we listen and obey.

THE TWO CRUCIAL QUESTIONS

The fictitious story of how Aslan restored Eustace to the original person God created him to be gives us nonfictional insights into how God can help restore us in the same way. The core issue in this whole unlayering process comes down to two questions: How does God see us? Are we loved, accepted, and forgiven by God? And the one-word answer: *Yes!* That's the core we all have to come back to so we can answer one more crucial question that comes next: *Do you believe this?*

To get to that point, to be *real*, we have to acknowledge the pain in our lives (maybe like a suddenly too-small gold bracelet that's become embedded in our arm as we've grown into a dragon).

Then we let God *peel* back the layers of dragon skin that we've added to our lives, perhaps due to destructive thoughts and habits—or perhaps with the best of intentions. This peeling process may "hurt like billy," as Eustace said. It hurts to break addictions or change habits or come face to face with the things that injured us in the first place.

Ah, but as those layers come away, we *feel* so much better—free of the layers that imprisoned us, free to celebrate the wonderful creation God designed us to be.

And then we *heal*. That healing is a whole new, ongoing process, one in which we're more aware of the decisions that continually confront us and in which we're better prepared to choose to head in the way that brings us closer to God with each breath we take.

Real.

Peel.

Feel.

Heal.

We *learn* to make this choice. Sometimes we learn the hard way—which may seem at first like the *easier* way until we wake up and realize we've turned into a dragon.

Here's another way to remember how we can *slay* the dragon we've become: we wield God's *sword* of truth, we find the dragon's *lair* (that is, we identify the *layer*), we *attack* the dragon, and, we say *yes!* to the truth. Get it? To slay the dragon, remember:

S—sword of truth
L—find the lair (layer)
A—attack the dragon
Y—say *yes!* to the truth

THE CONTAGION—AND CONQUERING— OF "DRAGONRY"

In this book I've shared some of the unhealthy or destructive ways I've layered myself with dragon skin over the years— with food in response to childhood abuse, with poor choices in response to temptation, and with selfishness instead of sharing. These are struggles I deal with on a daily basis, sometimes a minute-to-minute basis. Yet I know that to those who are dealing with struggles such as life-and-death addictions, it may seem silly to even mention a problem with chocolate chip cookies.

I've shared my story, hoping it helps you see that sometimes something that seems silly is actually lay-

> ❧
>
> *Most of the time, these destructive behaviors are hiding some hurtful incident or belief . . . that has caused someone to pull on layers of temporary pleasure, comfort, or protection.*

ering a hard hurt that goes all the way to the center of us, affecting every part of our lives. On the surface, it may seem simple, like a chocolate chip cookie—or the little gold bracelet from the treasure trove in the dragon's lair that Eustace slipped on his arm. But the cookie becomes a body layer, and the bracelet becomes a painful tourniquet; both cause us hurt and anguish, and we need to peel them so that nothing prevents us from having a close, authentic, truthful relationship with God and with those we love here on earth.

I'm inspired by how some people are able, with God's help, not only to escape from the hard layers that have resulted from childhood injuries and difficult times but also, eventually, to use those layers as tools to draw others to their own stories of redemption. I'm talking about *really* hard psychological or behavioral layers such as addiction to drugs, sex, pornography, gambling, compulsive shopping, overeating, undereating, and drinking too much alcohol . . . You know what I mean: the kinds of behaviors that fracture families and destroy lives.

Most of the time, these destructive behaviors are hiding some hurtful incident or belief, probably from years earlier, that has caused someone to pull on layers of temporary pleasure, comfort, or protection.

It's like escaping a storm by crawling into a dragon's lair and laying claim to the stolen treasure we find there. Before we know it, we've become a dragon too.

In contrast, there's the story of Tracy Elliot, who in her book *Unbroken* tells the story of her pain-packed childhood as an orphan reared in the projects by a grandmother whose household also included Tracy's five alcoholic uncles. Tracy witnessed constant violence and experienced repeated abuse throughout her growing-up years, and when she left home, headed into her own lair of addiction and bad choices. She became an alcoholic, a cocaine addict, and then a stripper.

Her book tells the amazing and inspiring story of how she finally fell down before God and let Him peel back those deadly layers of her life. Against all odds and only through God's grace, she became the original, abundantly blessed *Tracy* God had created her to be. She is married to a loving, prosperous businessman, and they have two beloved sons. In addition, Tracy was recently crowned Mrs. Texas.

With all this going for her, you might be surprised to learn that today Tracy is back out on the streets among the hopeless and the homeless. Uh-huh. But this time she's out there distributing bundles of sleeping bags, toiletries, and restaurant and grocery gift cards.

A PAST OF POOR CHOICES
AND HARD LAYERS

Tracy and I share the same amazement when we look back at our poor choices and hard layers. She says, "One of the great things about God is that He can and will use your screwups in life to make you stronger."[2]

Amen, sister! We've both experienced firsthand how

hard-layered "dragons" can roar through life, lashing out and hurting others as they suffer the consequences of destructive life choices and/or devastating addictions. Those hard layers may come, as they did for Tracy and me, as we seek psychological protection from a childhood injury or abusive situation. I'm eternally grateful that my poor choices didn't lead me into addiction, at least not the same ones as Tracy endured. I have my own set of compulsive behaviors, thank you. But I understand how addiction occurs, one choice at a time.

I understand how addiction occurs, one choice at a time.

Drugs ease the pain of remembering the bad thing that happened, and at the same time they can make the person so unpleasant or scary or dangerous to be with that relationships—and sometimes lives—are destroyed.

Often there's a terrible corollary that comes into play between addicts and the families and friends who are closest to them. Sometimes these friends and family members seem to catch the contagion of the dragon's hard, knobby, protective skin and start protecting themselves with hard layers too.

The beloved country music star June Carter Cash was a heart-wrenching example of how, unless we're especially diligent—and especially aware of the way each choice we make leads us in either the right or wrong direction—this can happen even when we're aware of the danger. In his amazingly personal biography of his mother's life, *Anchored in Love*, John Carter Cash describes how June watched, heartbroken, as her husband, Johnny Cash, and all of their children at one time or another over the years layered themselves with drug addiction.

June surely vowed she would never stumble into that drug-dependent dragon's lair herself, but toward the end of her life, that's exactly what happened. June became addicted to prescription drugs. To hard-layer the physical pain of her body as well as the emotional pain of her heart, she chose to take prescription medications—too many of them, more than she should have taken. And before she knew it, she had ended up in the dragon's lair of drug addiction herself.

Somehow, sooner or later, those who end up behind these hard layers inevitably become aware of what has happened to them. John Carter describes how he tried to confront his mother with her destructive dependency. At that point, June, like all of us, was one choice away from heading in the right direction. Sadly, the choice she made took her in the opposite direction.[3]

THE HARD LAYERS OF DENIAL

Another woman I know of also caught the contagion of hard layers in response to her child's self-destruction. She didn't join him in drug addiction. Instead she layered herself with the hard layers of denial. And by doing so, she became his most powerful enabler.

Like many of us who end up in the dragon's lair of hard layers, the woman got there after some incredibly hurtful experiences. Her husband left her to rear two sons alone (a third son was in college when he left). Their father's leaving was heartbreaking for the boys; they were devastated. Making matters worse, the dad immediately jumped into his new lifestyle as a happy-go-lucky bachelor who gave little attention to his sons. It wasn't at all unusual for him to tell them he was coming to pick them up for a visit . . . and then not show up.

In response to the pain she saw her sons enduring, the woman layered herself up with a supermom cape and tried to be everything to

The woman layered herself up with a supermom cape and tried to be everything to everyone.

everyone in her care. Part of her response came as she saw the hurt in her sons' eyes that their father had left them, and part of it came because of the guilt she felt about the role she played in her failed marriage that took that father from them.

The woman's oldest son in college got along fine, but the two boys at home were constantly in trouble. When the older of the two boys got a girl pregnant and dropped out of high school to marry her, the woman and her youngest son were left at home, just the two of them. Blaming herself for the older son's poor choices and the life-changing consequences, she became more determined than ever to protect her youngest son from his own hard choices.

She did her best, but the boy—I'll call him Mason, though that isn't his name—wanted a father. Unfortunately, his father seemed to have little interest in spending time with him. Mason's grades went down, and he started getting in trouble at school. His mother's first reactions—blaming the other kids for the fights, blaming the teachers for his poor grades—may have arisen out of her own tattered sense of pride. It's embarrassing when your child gets in trouble and doesn't do well in school while other parents adorn their cars with bumper stickers that tell the world how successful their kids are. ("My daughter is an A+ student in kindergarten!" "My son is on the honor roll in the Mensa School for the Gifted and Talented!")

Things got worse as the years passed. As a young teen, Mason ran with the wrong crowd, started doing drugs, and ended up in one mess after another. And every time he messed up, his mother rushed to "fix" the situation. She covered up for him, quickly picked him up whenever the police called, and continued to blame everyone else for her son's problems. She had good intentions, but her behavior was actually a layering of lies that ignored the truth and let her son escape any consequences for what he had done.

Layer by layer—guilt, self-blame, busyness, and embarrassment—she took on all the boy's problems and became the ultimate enabler. She bailed him out of jail, lied on his behalf to excuse his behavior, and pretended that each and every calamity was her fault.

But her enabling only made things worse as enabling

always does. While she was layering herself in response to the parenting and relational failures she perceived in herself, Mason was layering himself with behaviors aimed at burying the hurt he felt over his parents' abandonment. That's right. They both abandoned him—his father by leaving and his mother by layering herself away from him as an enabler. Those layers kept her from having an honest and real relationship with him.

By the time Mason was an adult, he had never had to feel the total weight of his destructive decisions, never had to suffer the consequences of his actions because his mother had always rushed in to make everything right. She saw that he always had what he needed, even if it meant she had to go without. Whenever he hit bottom, she listened to him cry, helped him clean up, gave him a place to live— and enabled him to hit bottom again.

Mason is middle-aged now and was recently released from prison. Now that he's graying around the temples, he's finally growing up. He is learning to take responsibility for his choices, but he's also making better choices than he ever has before.

I'm also happy to add that his mother is now—finally!— emerging from her own dragon's lair of hard emotional and psychological layers. With God's help, she is peeling back those enabler layers that grew as she tried to cover up her guilt and pain. Now she's becoming the grace-bathed woman and mother God created her to be. Finally she's acknowledging that, yes, her broken marriage impacted her children, but ultimately, her son's choices were not her fault but his, and he needed to bear the weight of responsibility for the choices he made.

CHOOSING TO LEARN HARD LESSONS

This woman's story reminds me of some powerful wisdom Patsy Clairmont shared about how we actually *disable* our children when we constantly *enable* them to repeat poor life choices. Patsy said, "Within the consequences of our children's choices is the curriculum that will cause them to mature. We so frequently rob them of those lessons when we rescue them, impeding them of the very growth we long for them to experience."

> *We actually disable our children when we constantly enable them to repeat poor life choices.*

Like many of us, this woman and her son chose to learn an important lesson the hard way. Now, that's not what they thought they were doing with each choice they made; it's undoubtedly not what they intended to do. But each time they were confronted with a potentially unpleasant situation, they could choose how they would respond. In every situation, they were one choice away from heading in the right direction . . . or turning down Hard-Lesson Lane.

For better or for worse, we often take our family members and friends right along with us as we make those choices throughout each day . . . throughout our lives. And the fact is, we've all learned hard lessons and added hard layers to our lives through poor choices along the way. As one quipster said, "We can't all learn by example. Sometimes it's our turn to be the example others learn from."

Sometimes it may seem that our decisions are too minor to matter to anyone but ourselves. But as Philip Yancey wrote, "The remarkable truth is that our choices matter, not just to us and our own destiny but, amazingly, to God Himself and the universe He rules."

Why would our everyday choices matter to God and to the universe? Well, the main reason is that He loves us and wants the best for us. All He asks of us is that we love Him and believe what He promises us. He has big plans for our lives (Jeremiah 29:11) and for the universe, but He doesn't cram those plans down our throats. No, instead He gave us a map, the Bible. Best of all, He sent His Son to earth to show us the way to Him—and to redeem us when our poor choices send us stumbling off in the wrong direction.

He invites us into a personal relationship with Him—a close, warm, nurturing, *wonderful* relationship with Him, with nothing standing between us and our Creator. No layers of shame, fear, guilt, or anything else. Right now . . . and every moment of our lives . . . we're one choice away from moving in that direction.

So what do I need now?

I need to remember, in every situation, that I'm one choiceawayfrompressingmyself closertoGod'sheart . . . or turning away from Him. In every situation, I want to choose to be God's representative to a hurting world.

So what do you need now?

I need _____

_____

_____

_____

_____

Every Day Is My Birthday

*If anyone is in Christ, he is a new creation;
the old has gone, the new has come!*

—2 CORINTHIANS 5:17

As an icebreaker at Women of Faith Association gatherings before each conference, Luci Swindoll asks the speakers thought-provoking questions designed to give association members an inside look at our personalities. We have to be on our toes because Luci's questions, different each time, really make us think.

One week she asked Anita Renfroe, "Anita, if you had to design a button that described your life using only five words, what would it say?"

Frankly, if Luci had asked me that question, the first button that popped into my mind might have said, "Which way to the food?" or "What time do we eat?" But Anita came right back with a completely different answer: "Every day is my birthday!" she said with a wide smile.

I love Anita, but honestly, I was expecting a deeper

answer from her. She's so bright, so witty, and so full of love for God, I guess I just thought she might come up with something a little more profound. Still, Anita's witty button slogan stayed with me. (And, come to think of it, that's what those buttons are supposed to do, right?)

Not too long after that, I celebrated my birthday. It was a great day, beginning with breakfast with Don followed by a fun car-pool trip with Sam and a friend to the golf driving range. During the drive, Don called me and said as soon as I had dropped off the boys at the driving range, I was to go immediately to the day spa because he had scheduled a massage for me. I loved that!

The day passed pleasantly, and that night my family treated me to a birthday dinner at my favorite Mexican restaurant where the mariachi band sang "Happy Birthday" to me in Español. To cap off the night, the entire family, including the kids, my parents, Don, and me, went to see the movie *Transformers*.

My birthday was a wonderful day, a time when I truly felt special and loved—what a great feeling. And since it was my special day, I felt like I could take a guilt-free nap or eat a guilt-free cookie or be silly if I wanted to or share a deep thought if I wanted to. It was my birthday, so I felt free to be myself without fear of guilt or judgment.

When I thought about it, I realized that if I enjoy those feelings only on my birthday, I must live the other 364 days of the year layered with self-condemnation. Yuck!

So . . . I got to work on those layers. Every day, I practice being the *me* I think I am on my birthday. I like her a lot.

Every day, I practice being the me *I think I am on my birthday. I like her a lot.*

Thank you, dear Anita, for giving me a button I want to mentally wear every day of my life. I apologize for thinking at first that it was a rather shallow thought for such a rich life as you and I both lead. It's actually a phenomenal slogan, and I hope you won't mind if I make it my own.

And since every day is my birthday, and every day is a new start, that means there's no end in sight. My life, like this book, is a work in progress. Every day I learn something new. Every morning is a fresh start, a second chance, a rebirth. And because I'm a Christian and plan to live forever, I know that even death itself isn't the end. Instead we simply go from life . . . to life eternal.

CELEBRATING THE ORIGINAL ME

Wearing that mental birthday button, I'm reminded every day to peel back my imprisoning layers and celebrate the original *me* God created me to be. The birthday button also takes my thoughts back to another button idea that's stuck with me ever since a friend shared it a couple of years ago. It's such a powerful image, I can't get it out of my mind.

It's an image that comes from Nathaniel Hawthorne's classic novel, *The Scarlet Letter*. In the story, Hester Prynne, a "fallen woman" during Colonial times, is forced by her Puritan community to wear the red letter A on the bodice of her dress as punishment for the sin of bearing a child out of wedlock.

My friend imagined that big scarlet letter A being worn by all the women today "who feel unworthy to hold their heads up as God's daughters." Now, thinking about that image, let me ask you: Are you one of us? If you are, what does that A stand for? Abuse? Adultery? Abortion? Appetite? Anger? Abandonment? Avoidance? Adoption? Alcohol?

Maybe it did originally. But now, as we come toward the end of this book, I hope you'll see instead that as Christians that A stands for something altogether different: *atonement*.

How could we have forgotten? All those mistakes we made, all those sins we committed are forgiven and forgotten, paid for in full by Jesus' death on the cross. And because of another wonderful A-word—*arisen!*—we have the promise of a gloriously wonderful life in heaven with God—*always*.

As in, *forever*.

Jesus paid the price for all our ugly *actions*. Our lives have been *atoned for*. So now we need to let God help us peel away those layers we've wrapped around our lives to hide our A-list sins and show the world instead the original beloved *angels* He created us to be. Well, maybe not *actual angels*. But in His eyes, we are downright *angelic*—beloved, cherished, and *adored*.

Let's learn to see ourselves as God sees us. When we do, we'll celebrate a new beginning every day. We'll feel like every day is our birthday.

Dr. Henry Cloud is a clinical psychologist who knows a lot about the way we layer ourselves away from who God created us to be. He refers to those layers with an image that makes me smile every time I think of it. When I heard him speak last year, he asked the audience, so insightfully, "What are you hiding behind your fig leaf?"

> *Let's learn to see ourselves as God sees us.*

God made us to be naked and without shame, Dr. Cloud said, but ever since the Fall when Adam and Eve disobeyed God in the Garden of Eden, we've been "faking it behind the fig leaf."

Don't you love that?

STEP OUT IN FAITH

We've been hiding our real, honest selves—our feelings, our dreams, the way we'd *like* to live our lives full of obvious, outward faith and trust in God's promises—behind fear, guilt, shame, condemnation, and a host of other fig-leafy layers. But Dr. Cloud says—and I'm sharing my own spin on how his words rang true for me—we need to dig up those hurtful things we've done or had done to us and acknowledge our sin or the way others' sins may have impacted us in negative ways. Then, he says, we must step out in faith—come out from behind that fig-leaf layer—to rediscover and celebrate the original free-and-joyful creation God intended us to be.

He acknowledges, as I've experienced firsthand, that this de-leafing process isn't easy and can be flat-out scary. There's always the possibility that we'll finally allow others to see the real us . . . and they'll snarl and say they prefer the old, layered-up version.

Or maybe a friend will say, after you've lost weight, that you look sickly or unhealthy now. Maybe while you're battling some addiction, someone will whine, "Oh come on. One little _____ won't hurt." Maybe a family member will argue, "But you always laughed when I told that story every Christmas about how you wet your pants at church that Sunday. Now you're saying you don't want me to tell it because it *embarrasses you*?"

Dr. Cloud says that in order to grow, we have to "take a step past where we've been." Take a step, he says, that's unpleasant or that scares you to death.

Do it boldly with steadfast faith that the God who created you is powerful enough to get you through that next step . . . and the next.

I know, I know. That's big talk for someone like me who's acknowledged a whole wardrobe of hard-to-peel layers. But let me tell you about a couple of ways I've carried out Dr. Cloud's advice, along with the other thoughts

I've learned about layering by personal experience—the thoughts I've shared with you in this book.

Let's go back to that photo shoot I described in chapter 4 and the dreaded proofs I knew would be coming in the mail. Encouraged by the positive attitude I'd enjoyed during the shoot itself, I pictured those proofs landing on my doorstep. I thought about it, tossing my choices around my mind. Finally I called Pat and told her, "I'm going to look at the proofs."

"Good for you, Sandi!" she said. "You look at them, and when you do, I hope you'll feel love for the woman you see in them. See her through God's eyes."

And that's what I did. I settled down with those proofs at the kitchen counter (making sure the scissors were well out of reach), and I looked at those unretouched, unairbrushed pictures with love as Pat suggested. That simple act helped me peel back the layers of condemnation and shame so that I could appreciate the Sandi who's been hiding underneath them for so long, the Sandi God created me to be. Amazingly, when I looked at the pictures with God's eyes, I thought I heard Him say in my heart, *You know, I did a darn good job!*

I may be a slow learner about this layering stuff . . . but I *am* learning. And I've learned a lot from watching others. One of them is my daughter, Erin. She has just emerged as a beautiful young lady after that awkward adolescent stage all kids go through. Recently she got some proofs back too—her senior pictures.

In the past she's been a little bit too much like her mother when she's looked at pictures of herself. She never took the scissors to them, as far as I know, but she had trouble seeing anything good in them even though the rest of her family was quick to contradict her.

Last year, about the time I was going through my own ordeal with the album-cover proofs, Erin got the proofs of her senior pictures. She sat at the kitchen counter and pulled them out of the envelope. She sat there quietly, looking through them one by one, then she looked up at me and said, "Mom . . . I love these!"

I ran around the counter to look at the proofs over her shoulder, and there in those pictures I saw my beautiful Erin—the same one I had seen every day of her life and in every photo that had ever been taken of her. It was such a lesson for me! God had peeled away that layer of adolescent attitude, and now Erin was seeing herself through her adoring mother's eyes—and through her Creator's eyes—to acknowledge the gorgeous girl He had created her to be.

My own experience, and my experience with Erin and *her* proofs, reminded me of that quote from Henry David Thoreau: "It's not what you look at that matters," he said. "It's what you see."

QUESTIONING MYSELF
ABOUT HOARDING: HWMB?

Here's that second little *scary* step I've taken as I've worked at peeling back my layers. Remember how I admitted earlier to having a layer of hoarding? This defensive strategy is more than hoarding snack bars "just in case" I somehow get on the wrong flight and end up in a starvation-plagued Third World country. You'll remember I've also realized that I hoard myself: my time, my friendship—and also my *friendliness* when I'm among strangers.

As a Christian, I want to have my radar turned on when I'm traveling so I'm alert to any divine appointments God may have set up for me. On the other hand, I do have some inherent shyness in my personality; it's not my nature to move through a crowd of strangers, shaking hands and introducing myself unless that's absolutely called for in the public gatherings I attend.

Usually what I do on all those airplanes I fly on is just sit there and sleep or read. So as soon as I plop into my seat, I usually open up my book or magazine and become (or pretend to be) totally focused on what I'm reading. Maybe I excuse my isolating behavior by reminding myself how overzealous Christians can sometimes do more harm than good when they start spouting Scripture and preaching to every person they encounter. But more often I'm simply hoarding myself again, stepping back from connecting to other people.

I wanted to work on this layer, so I resolved to take that next unpleasant step Dr. Cloud described. To get started, before I got on that next plane, I asked myself one simple question: how would Marilyn be? As long as I've known her, I've admired Marilyn Meberg's nonintrusive friendliness. Watching her in action is a lesson in living an unlayered life.

I want to have my radar turned on when I'm traveling so I'm alert to any divine appointments God may have set up for me.

It starts with her body language. Marilyn stands tall, sits up straight, smiles often, and has a hair-trigger laugh. Everyone who knows Marilyn loves being with her, and the primary reason we feel that way is that she's *real*. When you're with Marilyn, you feel like you're with the real deal. She comes across as someone who readily acknowledges her flaws and shortcomings, her disappointments and hurts, but who confidently moves through life as one who's constantly aware that she is layered in grace by her Creator, who loves and adores her just the way she is—just the way He created her.

Buoyed by that confidence, when Marilyn talks to people, she looks them right in the eye.

So that's why, when I'm working on that hoarding layer, I ask myself that question before I get on an airplane. Here's what I've seen Marilyn do: She settles into her seat, smiles at her seatmate, and then with a strong, confident, and pleasant voice, she says hello and maybe asks two or three questions: "How are you? Where are you going today? Are you leaving home or going home?"

Now, I also happen to know that Marilyn has her own book or magazine ready to read. She's not inviting the person to talk nonstop for three hours on a cross-country flight. And yet she's connecting, letting that man or woman know she works for Women of Faith and making herself approachable in case God put that seat-mate there for a special reason. After a pleasant round of back-and-forth, she smiles, pulls out her book, and starts reading.

None of us want to get trapped by a TMI (too much information) motor-mouth who can't stop talking and shares details about everything from toe hair to cup size while showing off her sixty-two-page photo album from the last visit with the grandkids. So there *is* a need for boundaries there. On the other hand, I do want to be friendly and ready for whatever God has in mind. I'm inspired when I hear of the amazing conversations and experiences the Women of Faith staff and team members have had, not only with the audiences of thousands who attend the conferences but also with hotel maids, arena ushers, caterers, hotel van drivers—and airplane seat-mates. Those experiences come when we peel back the layers that "protect" us from being real.

MAKING PEACE WITH WHAT HURTS

Earlier I shared how our family is handling the layers that came through that recent roller-coaster year of graduations, marriage, and the death of the Peslis kids' beloved mom. There was one more event during that time of emotional highs and heartaches that provided another poignant lesson in layering. Compared with a child losing his or her mother, it's such a trivial thing that I hesitated to mention it here. But it also shows how our family members are letting each other see beneath the layers to share our vulnerable hearts and real hurts.

In 1993, I took my kids, Anna, Jen, Jon, and Erin, to see the movie *Homeward Bound,* the heartwarming story about two dogs and a cat who get lost from their owners and undertake an incredible journey to find their way home. In what had to be the world's smartest (and, in some parents' opinion, most underhanded) marketing move, the Humane Society had set up a little adoption center right there in front of the theater.

Our family members are letting each other see beneath the layers to share our vulnerable hearts and real hurts.

The kids immediately started in on me, begging to adopt a puppy. I hustled everyone into the theater, thinking they would forget about the puppies when the movie started. And sure enough, they got so absorbed in the story I didn't get any of the whispered pleas or elbow nudges I'd been expecting.

But *I* couldn't forget the puppies! While the kids were engrossed in the movie, I slipped away to check out the details of the adoption program. After talking to the Humane Society staff and looking at the adorable puppies, I returned to my seat thinking, *If the kids ask again on our way out, I'll let them do it.*

Well, of course, they did. And as we gathered around the puppy pen trying to decide which one to adopt, this one little guy put his paws through the holes in the mesh, trying to get to us.

No question about it, he was the one for us.

On the way home we discussed names, and Jonathan said, "Well, he's got brown hair. How about if we call him Brownie?" The other kids thought that was perfect, and that's how we ended up with our feisty little mutt.

Brownie only weighed about five pounds, but he had the attitude of a cocky canine who could have been named Big Dog Studley. He wouldn't hurt a thing—but he didn't want anyone to know it. He could hear an envelope being dropped into a mailbox, a car turning into our driveway, or a neighborhood friend stepping up to our front door long before anyone else knew what was happening, and he would let us know of the impending invasion with excitement that others might have reserved for the Starship *Enterprise* landing on our front lawn.

Although he loved us all, Brownie's favorite, hands-down, was Jonathan. Somehow the two of them bonded in a very special way. Then a couple of years after the kids and I adopted Brownie, Don and I married, and our families merged for that chaotically joyful life in the blender. Brownie welcomed our new family members and quickly accepted them into the circle of people he was committed to love and protect.

Then we adopted Sam, and Brownie made room in his

little heart for a whole new duty: babysitter. We would put Sam on a blanket on the floor to kick and squirm, and Brownie would sidle up next to him, like a pint-size Doberman, and growl if anyone he didn't know came close! He loved Sam right from the beginning.

When Sam was seven or so, he fell in love with a puppy at a neighbor's house, and we all agreed we needed to adopt it too. Soon the puppy grew into a lovable coffee-table-sized pooch Sam named Lucky. Brownie wasn't too crazy about this newcomer, but it may have had something to do with the fact that, when he grew up, Lucky sometimes carried Brownie around by Brownie's Invisible Fencing collar, sort of like a woman carrying a purse. I know it must have been humiliating for little Brownie; he snarled and snapped at Lucky while Lucky happily carried him off somewhere, and then the two would play together.

Well, the years passed, and last year Brownie turned fifteen. You know, that's equivalent to 105 in people years. Brownie gradually had become as feeble as a crippled little old man. He couldn't hear, couldn't see, couldn't get his back legs to work most of the time, and he developed what we delicately described as *incontinence issues*.

We all talked about what would be best for Brownie. He was obviously miserable, and we came to the unanimous decision that he had suffered enough. I made an appointment with the vet to have him put to sleep.

Oh, what a traumatic thing that was for us, especially coming as it did so quickly after the even more agonizing heart-hurt of Michelle's death, which had come just two weeks after her own father's death. So Don's kids had lost their grandfather and mother within a month of each other. As we talked to the kids about who would go to the vet's office with Brownie, we gently excused Donnie, Mollie, and Aly from even considering adding this fresh new burden onto their hearts.

Don was willing to go it alone if the rest of us just couldn't bear the thought of doing it. But in the end, the group included Jonathan, Sam, Don, and me along with Don's biological dad, our wonderful Pop, who was visiting from West Virginia and determined to be with his grandsons during this ordeal.

On the day of the appointment, we gently carried Brownie to the car. On the way to the vet's office, we stopped by our old house where we had lived when we adopted Brownie and for several years afterward. He had loved chasing squirrels around the big lawn of that home, and we thought . . . well, I don't know what we thought. Maybe we were offering him a farewell tour. Maybe we were just stalling.

We pulled into the driveway of the house and eased him out onto the grass. He stood there a minute, sniffing the air and looking around through his tired old eyes. Then he hobbled over to the mud-room entryway where he'd always gone in and out of the house and scratched at the bottom of the door to be let in, just as he had done so many years ago.

The veterinarian asked if we wanted to leave Brownie—or stay with him until the end. We all opted to stay, standing by the table where he lay as he drifted off to a final sleep. We stroked him and told him what a good dog he'd been. Sam thanked him for being a good friend to Lucky, and Jonathan thanked him for being such a good squirrel-chaser. Surrounded by his favorite boys and most devoted grown-ups, Brownie licked our hands a few times, thumped his tail a time or two, then closed his eyes and seemed to relax into a painless death.

> *We were with family, and we felt comfortable peeling back those "put-on-a-good-face" layers and just letting our true heartache show.*

Here's the thing I so appreciated about my family that day: we *all* cried. Jonathan managed to hold it together until we got back in the car, but the rest of us, Don and Pop included, were wiping away our tears and blowing our noses and letting our sorrow show throughout that long afternoon. We didn't hold back. Didn't try to be "strong," no matter how mature or "manly" anyone in the group pretended to be the rest of the time. We were with family, and we felt comfortable peeling back those put-on-a-good-face layers and just letting our true heartache show.

UN-LAYERING OURSELVES BEFORE GOD

As I said earlier, it does seem trivial to even mention a family pet's death in the same story describing the loss of two

beloved members of the family—a mother and a grandfather. But that's what unlayering ourselves before the Lord
means. Psalm 56:8 says, "You've kept track of my every toss
and turn through the sleepless nights, each tear entered in your
ledger, each ache written in your book" (MSG). It doesn't say,
"You've kept track of the tears I've cried for *big* reasons." It
says *each* tear . . . *each* ache . . . *every* toss and turn.

It doesn't do any good to hide our feelings behind protective layers of disguises or fake feelings. God sees *all* our
tears, *all* our true feelings. When we wrap ourselves in layers
of behaviors or thoughts to hide our
real selves from Him, we're just rob-
bing ourselves of the warm, enrich-
ing, encouraging embrace of love
and grace He wants to give us.

God sees all our tears,
all our true feelings.

I've known many people who,
when they're hurt or scared, lash
out at those who try to comfort them. Whether their hearts
are broken by the death of a loved one or the loss of a pet,
they turn a cold shoulder to anyone who tries to come
alongside them and cry with them. They remind me of my
friend's dog who was hit by a car. She ran to her beloved
pet to help him, but as she dropped down beside him on the
street and reached out to pet him, he bit her!

She was shocked that this pet that had been so devoted to
her for so long would lash out at her that way. The dog was acting the same way any of us might react if we were hiding our
own hurts and heartache with a hard layer of self-protection.

Not too long ago, I heard someone say something that instantly took me back to the woman whose injured dog bit her. He said, "We're all either wounded healers—or unhealed wounders. It just depends on which side of the river we're on."

We're all wounded, one way or another. We all suffer hurts throughout our lives. And we're all just one choice away from the light or the darkness. In his 1959 book *Man's Search for Meaning,* concentration camp survivor Viktor Frankl wrote that our suffering by itself is meaningless, but we *give* it meaning "by the way in which we respond to it."[1] Our response determines which side of the river we're on, as the other man said.

We're all just one choice away from the light or the darkness.

In his foreword to the 2006 edition of Frankl's book (the book has sold more than twelve million copies since it was published nearly fifty years ago), Rabbi Harold Kushner wrote that everything you possess can be taken from you "except one thing, your freedom to choose how you will respond to the situation. You cannot control what happens to you in life, but you can always control what you will feel and do about what happens to you."[2]

This choosing is another ongoing process. We choose how we react to the situations that confront us every day—including those who, like the woman's injured dog, act out their woundedness in unexpected ways—like anger. It's a phenomenon expressed by another one of those grammatical oddities where the same words mean more than one thing. In this case, "Hurt people hurt people." When someone lashes out at us unexpectedly, we can choose how we respond. We can choose, as Grandma Grace did when she baked the cherry pie, to consider what hurt might be hiding beneath that outward layer of hatefulness. Then we can choose whether to respond in anger ourselves, perpetuating the hatefulness, or we can choose to show the same grace and mercy our God extends to us.

GOD'S SONG IN US

God created us to love Him and to love one another. He made each one of us unique, with the specific personality and appearance—the specific DNA—He wanted us to have. We are His beloved creations! How frustrating it must be to Him when we hide that creation behind layers of shame, guilt, addiction, anger, abuse . . . whatever.

My goal in this book has been to bring you along on my ongoing journey of removing the layers that keep me from being the woman God created me to be—that keep me from being as close as I can be to Him, heart to heart. Maybe along the way you've discovered layers of your own life that are holding you back from that kind of thrilling and *real* relationship with Him. Well, remember girlfriend: every day—including *today*—*is* our birthday, our fresh start, second chance, new beginning. Today's the day we're gonna get to work on peeling away those layers so we can heal and get real.

I've heard that creative scientists have learned how to take a person's DNA structure and make music out of it. Frankly, I wouldn't know a double helix from a daffodil, but I do know music, and I love knowing that my DNA, which is like no other DNA in the whole wide world, is also a song like no one else's.

> *God, the Creator of the universe, sings to me. And to you.*

God not only created me, He wrote a song in me! And I believe He sings that song to me every day of my life. Zephaniah 3:17 says, "The LORD your God is with you, he is mighty to save. He will take great delight in you, he will quiet you with his love, he will rejoice over you with singing."

Did you get that? God, the Creator of the universe, *sings* to me.

And to you.

When I first put this together in my mind, I thought, *Oh, I'd love to find some scientist who could turn my DNA into music for me, so I could hear my song. I'd love to know what it sounds like.*

And then it hit me. I may not know what the *music* sounds like, but I already know the words to the song God wrote in me. They're the same lyrics He wrote into *your* song but with different music: ridiculously simple and at the same time extraordinarily profound, and He sings them to us every moment of every day: "Haaaaaaapy birthday to you, happy birthday to you . . ."

Girlfriend, peel back the layers, listen for God's voice singing your song into your life, and rediscover the original, marvelous *you* He created you to be.

So what do I need now?

I need to sing!

"Is any one of you in trouble? He should pray. Is anyone happy? Let him sing songs of praise" (James 5:13). "I will praise the LORD all my life; I will sing praise to my God as long as I live" (Psalm 146:2).

So what do you need now?

I need _____

_____

_____

NO TURNING BACK NOW!

Even though the apostle Paul wrote these words, they are mine too—and, I hope, yours as well:

I'm not saying that I have this all together, that I have it made. But I am well on my way, reaching out for Christ, who has so wondrously reached out for me. Friends, don't get me wrong: By no means do I count myself an expert in all of this, but I've got my eye on the goal, where God is beckoning us onward—to Jesus. I'm off and running, and I'm not turning back.

—PHILIPPIANS 3:12–14 MSG

Sandi's Resources

BOOKS

Stephen Arterburn: *Healing Is a Choice*

Jerry Bridges: *The Pursuit of Holiness*

Dr. Henry Cloud: *Changes That Heal*

Tracy Elliott: *Unbroken*

R. T. Kendall: *Total Forgiveness*

Carol Kent: *When I Lay My Isaac Down*

Greg Laurie: *The God of the Second Chance*

Brennan Manning: *Ragamuffin Gospel* and *Abba's Child*

Marilyn Meberg: *Love Me, Never Leave Me*

Beth Moore: *When Godly People Do Ungodly Things*

Henri Nouwen: *Life of the Beloved* and *The Return of the Prodigal Son*

Patricia Raybon: *I Told the Mountain to Move*

Bev Smallwood: *This Wasn't Supposed to Happen to Me*

Philip Yancey: *What's So Amazing About Grace?* and *The Jesus I Never Knew*

COUNSELING RESOURCES

New Life Ministries
1-800-NEW-LIFE
www.newlife.com

Crossroads Christian Counseling
719-395-4673
www.crossroadscounseling.net

This counseling retreat center, set in the small mountain town of Buena Vista, Colorado, features brief, intensive treatment. It is staffed by believers with excellent counseling credentials. Several of my friends have gone there for intensives and have come back with glowing reviews of the help they received. There is real value in doing intensives over a short period of time, getting the help you need immediately, rather than dragging out the process for a year or more.

Remuda Ranch
1-800-445-1900
www.remudaranch.com

Remuda Ranch provides biblically based intensive inpatient and residential programs for women and girls suffering from eating disorders and related issues.

PRAYER RESOURCES

Philippian Ministries
www.philippian.com
 Lana Bateman's Philippian Ministries is designed to bring
encouragement, growth, and healing for God's hurting children.

LIFE COACHING
AND LIFE PLANNING

Nearly all life coaching is done via telephone. Life plan-
ning is always done in person, often in intensive sessions
of eight hours or more.

My own life coach and friend is Carolyn Gill:
www.carolyngillcoaching.com.

Carol Travilla and Joan Webb:
www.intentionalwoman.com

Find a list of certified life planners at
www.purposedrivenlife.com/pathfinders/lpfacilitators.
aspx. These are Christian life planners certified under
the Tom Paterson process, affiliated with Rick Warren's
Saddleback Church.

Find a list of Christian coaches at
www.christiancoaches.com.

Christopher McCluskey is a Christian coach who teaches
and trains other Christian coaches. His Web site is full of
useful information: www.christian-living.com.

Sandi's Layer-Peelers

These are some of the Scripture passages I've shared in this book as being especially helpful to me as I've peeled back the destructive layers of my life. I recommend that you memorize your favorites or copy them onto index cards that you place around your home or carry in your car.

Seek first the kingdom of God and His righteousness, and all these things shall be added to you.

—Matthew 6:33 NKJV

Pure grace and nothing but grace be with all who love our Master, Jesus Christ.

—Ephesians 6:24 MSG

I gave up all that inferior stuff so I could know Christ personally, experience his resurrection power, be a partner in his suffering, and go all the way with him to death itself.

—Philippians 3:10–11 MSG

This is the real and eternal life: That they know you, the one and only true God, and Jesus Christ, whom you sent.

—John 17:3 MSG

For it is by grace you have been saved, through faith—and this not from yourselves, it is the gift of God.

—Ephesians 2:8

Your beauty should not come from outward adornment . . . Instead, it should be that of your inner self.

—1 Peter 3:3–4

And my God will meet all your needs according to his glorious riches in Christ Jesus.

—Philippians 4:19

I praise you because I am fearfully and wonderfully made; your works are wonderful, I know that full well.

—Psalm 139:14

If we love one another, God dwells deeply within us, and his love becomes complete in us—perfect love!

—1 John 4:12 MSG

It is God who arms me with strength and makes my way perfect.

—2 Samuel 22:33

This is GOD's work. We rub our eyes—we can hardly believe it!

—Psalm 118:23 MSG

We all arrive at your doorstep sooner or later, loaded with guilt.

—Psalm 65:2 MSG

I remind you, my dear children: Your sins are forgiven in Jesus' name.

—1 John 2:12 MSG

Change your life. Turn to God and be baptized, each of you, in the name of Jesus Christ, so your sins are forgiven. Receive the gift of the Holy Spirit.

—Acts 2:38 MSG

But I'll take the hand of those who don't know the way, who can't see where they're going. I'll be a personal guide to them, directing them through unknown country. I'll be right there to show them what roads to take, make sure they don't fall into the ditch. These are the things I'll be doing for them—sticking with them, not leaving them for a minute.

—Isaiah 42:16 MSG

Generous in love—God, give grace! Huge in mercy—wipe out my bad record. Scrub away my guilt, soak out my sins in your laundry.

—Psalm 51:1–2 MSG

Unlike the culture around you, always dragging you down to its level of immaturity, God brings the best out of you.

—Romans 12:2 MSG

For you created my inmost being; you knit me together in my mother's womb. I praise you because I am fearfully and wonderfully made; your works are wonderful, I know that full well.

—Psalm 139:13–14

He who began a good work in you will carry it on to completion.

—Philippians 1:6

Oh LORD my God, I called to you for help and you healed me.

—Psalm 30:2

I do not understand what I do. For what I want to do I do not do, but what I hate I do.

—Romans 7:15

We do not know what we ought to pray for, but the Spirit himself intercedes for us with groans that words cannot express.

—Romans 8:26

Whether you turn to the right or to the left, your ears will hear a voice behind you, saying, "This is the way; walk in it."

—Isaiah 30:21

For we do not have a high priest who is unable to sympathize with our weaknesses, but we have one who has been tempted in every way, just as we are—yet was without sin.

—Hebrews 4:15

His powerful Word is sharp as a surgeon's scalpel, cutting through everything, whether doubt or defense, laying us open to listen and obey.

—Hebrews 4:12 MSG

If anyone is in Christ, he is a new creation; the old has gone, the new has come!

—2 Corinthians 5:17

I can do all things through Christ who strengthens me.

—Philippians 4:13 NKJV

The LORD your God is with you, he is mighty to save. He will take great delight in you, he will quiet you with his love, he will rejoice over you with singing.

—Zephaniah 3:17

Is any one of you in trouble? He should pray. Is anyone happy? Let him sing songs of praise.

—James 5:13

I will praise the LORD all my life; I will sing praise to my God as long as I live.

—Psalm 146:2

NOTES

CHAPTER 2: OUTSMARTING THE MIRROR

    1. Max Lucado, *You Are Special* (Wheaton, IL: Crossway Books, 1997).

CHAPTER 5: HEALING HURTS

    1. Madeline L'Engle, *And It Was Good: Reflections on Beginning*s (Colorado Springs: Shaw Books, 2000).

CHAPTER 6: UN-LAYERING LOVED ONES

    1. Marilyn Meberg, *Love Me, Never Leave Me* (Nashville: Thomas Nelson, Inc., 2008).

CHAPTER 7: ONE CHOICE AWAY . . .

    1. Francis Schaffer, *The God Who Is There* (Downers Grove, IL: InterVarsity, 1998).

CHAPTER 8: HARD LAYERS

    1. *The Voyage of the Dawn Treader* by C. S. Lewis © C. S. Lewis Pte. Ltd. 1952. Used with permission.

    2. Tracy Elliot, *Unbroken* (Nashville: Thomas Nelson, Inc., 2007).

    3. John Carter Cash, *Anchored in Love* (Nashville: Thomas Nelson, Inc., 2007).

NOT THE END: *EVERY DAY IS MY BIRTHDAY*

    1. Viktor Frankl, *Man's Search for Meaning* (Boston: Beacon Press, 2006).

    2. Ibid.

ABOUT THE AUTHOR

As one of the most highly acclaimed performers of our time with five Grammy awards, four Billboard Music Awards, three platinum records, five gold records, and eleven million units sold, Sandi Patty is simply known as "The Voice."

Sandi was introduced to the world with her rendition of "The Star-Spangled Banner" during the rededication of the Statue of Liberty in 1986. Virtually overnight she became one of the country's best-loved performers. Her version of the national anthem has become synonymous with patriotic celebration, including performances at "A Capitol Fourth" with the National Symphony, the Pan American Games, the Indianapolis 500, the dedication of the Francis Scott Key Memorial in Washington, D.C., the dedication of the Camp David Chapel, and ABC's Fourth of July Special.

Sandi is the most awarded female vocalist in contemporary music history. With thirty-nine Dove Awards, she was inducted into the Gospel Music Hall of Fame in 2004 and named an Indiana Living Legend in 2007. While her thirty-year career is heavily rooted in the gospel music industry, Sandi has had the opportunity in more recent years to extend her career outside the genre, performing with symphonies across the country, including the Boston Pops, Cincinnati Pops, Dallas Symphony, Baltimore Symphony, Houston Symphony, and Oklahoma City Philharmonic. Her first pops album, *An American Songbook*, was recorded with the London Symphony Orchestra.

In addition to her prolific musical career, Sandi is also an accomplished author. For the bestseller *Broken on the Back Row*, she received the 2006 Silver Angel Award. Her other titles include *Life in the Blender* and *Falling Forward*. Her down-to-earth style and strong common sense have endeared her to Women of Faith audiences. She's an example to all of us of the freedom that comes from discovering how to move on, learning from her mistakes, and letting God use her in any circumstance.

One of Sandi's dreams was to perform on Broadway, but her commitment to raising her family of eight children always came first. The Indianapolis Symphony Orchestra offered the best of both worlds with *Sandi Patty's Broadway*, her 2007 debut feature musical.

"I am grateful for the many opportunities God has given in my life and for how He has allowed me to spread my wings," says Sandi. "Singing is my way to tell my story of hope, life, and love." She and her family reside in Anderson, Indiana.

For more information about Sandi Patty, please visit www.sandipatty.com.

For bookings, please contact:
William Morris Agency
1600 Division Street, Suite 300, Nashville, TN 37203
615-963-3000

For management information, please contact:
Mike Atkins Entertainment
615-345-4554

SANDI PATTY

falling *forward*

...into His arms of grace

0849918863

Falling Forward welcomes us into Sandi's world of big families, busy tour schedules, conversations with women around the country, and personal conversations with God. While not telling us how to live, Sandi unfolds God's amazing creativity in using broken people to glorify Him.

Blending
Families, Lives,
and Relationships
with Grace

Life
in the
Blender

SANDI PATTY

Grammy Award Winner and Gospel Music Hall of Fame Inductee

0849900468

Whether it's in a blended family or in the daily struggle to keep balance between job and family, every woman experiences blending on some level. Drawing from her personal "his, mine, and ours" experience, Grammy Award–winning singer and Women of Faith speaker Sandi Patty provides insight on how to stay focused when life threatens to spin out of control.

WOMEN OF FAITH
INFINITE GRACE
CONFERENCE 2008

RELAX! Join us and learn why you can stop trying so hard. Come and see what it can mean to rest in God's amazing, unequaled, Infinite Grace!

Featuring the Women of Faith Team

PRE-CONFERENCE
Friday 9:00 AM - 3:00 PM
I Second That Emotion
Do your feelings have you tied in knots? You're not the only one! Join Patsy Clairmont, Anita Renfroe, and Jan Silvious for a day of laughter therapy and solid biblical teaching on understanding your emotions.

Coming to a City near YOU!

National Conference San Antonio, TX February 7 - 9	St. Louis, MO June 13 - 14	Kansas City, MO August 8 - 9	Portland, OR October 10 - 11
Omaha, NE March 28 - 29	East Rutherford, NJ June 20 - 21	Tampa, FL August 15 - 16	St. Paul, MN October 17 - 18
Little Rock, AR April 4 - 5	Seattle, WA June 27 - 28	Dallas, TX August 22 - 23	Houston, TX October 24 - 25
Fresno, CA April 11 - 12	Alaska Cruise Seattle, WA – Port City June 29 - July 6	Anaheim, CA September 5 - 6	Greensboro, NC October 31 - November 1
Spokane, WA April 18 - 19		Philadelphia, PA September 12 - 13	Ft. Lauderdale, FL November 7 - 8
Columbus, OH April 25 - 26	Washington, DC July 11 - 12	Denver, CO September 19 - 20	Oklahoma City, OK November 14 - 15
Jacksonville, FL May 16 - 17	Cleveland, OH July 18 - 19	Atlanta, GA September 26 - 27	Phoenix (Glendale), AZ November 21 - 22
Rochester, NY June 6 - 7	Boston, MA July 25 - 26	San Jose, CA October 3 - 4	
	Indianapolis, IN August 1 - 2		

"AND GOD IS ABLE TO MAKE ALL GRACE ABOUND TO YOU, THAT ALWAYS HAVING ALL SUFFICIENCY IN EVERYTHING, YOU MAY HAVE AN ABUNDANCE FOR EVERY GOOD DEED."
– II CORINTHIANS 9:8

Register NOW! Visit us at womenoffaith.com or call 888-49-FAITH

Dates, locations and speakers are subject to change. See registration deadlines at womenoffaith.com.